MW00471602

Rivers, Raiders, and Renegades

*True Stories about
Settlers, Soldiers, Indians, and Outlaws
on the Pennsylvania Frontier*

JOHN L. MOORE

SUNBURY
PRESS

Mechanicsburg, Pennsylvania USA

10/10/2018
R.L.S.

Published by Sunbury Press, Inc.
50 West Main Street
Mechanicsburg, Pennsylvania 17055

www.sunburypress.com

Copyright © 2003, 2014 by John L. Moore.
Cover copyright © 2014 by Sunbury Press.

ISBN: 978-1-62006-515-0 (Trade Paperback)
Library of Congress Control Number: 2014956356

FIRST SUNBURY PRESS EDITION: November 2014

Product of the United States of America
0 1 1 2 3 5 8 13 21 34 55

Set in Bookman Old Style
Designed by Lawrence Knorr
Cover by Lawrence Knorr
Cover Art "Warrior Bowman" by Andrew Knez, Jr.
Edited by Janice Rhayem

Continue the Enlightenment!

JOHN L. MOORE's

FRONTIER PENNSYLVANIA SERIES

Bows, Bullets, & Bears
Cannons, Cattle, & Campfires
Forts, Forests, & Flintlocks
Pioneers, Prisoners, & Peace Pipes
Rivers, Raiders, & Renegades
Settlers, Soldiers, & Scalps
Traders, Travelers, & Tomahawks
Warriors, Wampum, & Wolves

Author's Note on Quotations

I have taken a journalist's approach to writing about the people whose lives and experiences are chronicled in this book. Long dead, they nonetheless speak to us through the many letters, diaries, journals, official reports, depositions, interrogations, examinations, minutes, and memoirs that they left behind.

Whenever possible, I have presented the people I have written about in their own words. My intent is to allow the reader a sense of immediacy with historical figures who lived two or more centuries ago. To accomplish this, I have occasionally omitted phrases or sentences from quotations, and I have employed an ellipsis (...) to indicate where I have done so. In some instances, I have modernized punctuation; and in others, spelling has been modernized.

John L. Moore
Northumberland, PA
October 2014

Dedication

In memory of my father, the late
Leon H. Moore Jr.

Acknowledgments

My thanks to my wife, Jane E. Pritchard-Moore, for editing the manuscript. Thanks also to Robert B. Swift for making many valuable suggestions.

The People of the Rising Sun

Introduction

Once, the great rivers emptying into the Atlantic Ocean, known today as the Hudson and the Delaware, had different names. That was before the Europeans arrived in North America, and only the Indians lived along these huge waterways.

The Native Americans living along the lower reaches of these two rivers called the Hudson the Mohicannittuck after the Mohican Indians who dwelled a distance upriver. Their name for the Delaware was Lenapewihittuck, which meant River of the Lenape; and, in turn, Lenape was the short version of their name for themselves. Their full name was Lenni Lenape, or, as some of the earliest Europeans heard it, Renni Renappi. However their name was pronounced—most authorities believe it was Lenni Lenape—the words meant "The Original People," a name apparently stemming from their belief that they were the first people ever to inhabit the Eastern Seaboard in the vicinity of the Delaware and Hudson Rivers. The land between the two rivers the Lenape knew as Sheyichbi, which means, simply, "the land between the two rivers."

Other Indians living near the Sheyichbi knew the Lenape as "the grandfathers," and some of these neighboring bands believed they were somehow related to or descended from the Lenape. Indians living to the west of them referred to Sheyichbi as the land of the rising sun and called the Lenape the People of the Rising Sun.

Like most North American Indians, the Lenape had no written history and relied exclusively on oral

1

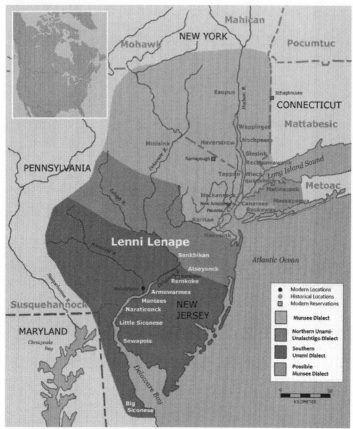

Lenapehoking, the original Lenape territory. Munsee speakers in the north,Unami-speakers in the center, and Unalichtigo-speakers in the south.

traditions to tell of the genesis of their people. One of the Europeans who knew them best said their tribal memory of their beginnings was vague and recalled only that once their ancestors had lived in the remote North American west, apparently far to the west of the Mississippi. The European, a missionary who took great pains to record these legends, said that for some reason the Lenape had since forgotten, their ancestors had migrated eastward in a body. At some point—but

DELAWARE INDIAN FAMILY.
[From Campanius' "New Sweden."]

only after many years of travel—some of their ancestors crossed the Mississippi, then the Allegheny Mountains, and eventually arrived at Sheyichbi. Because of the ocean, they could go no further east, and because no other people were living there when they arrived, these ancestors settled. These ancestors believed that God, or Mannitto, had intended and set aside the Sheyichbi country for them. When the

Europeans first came, the descendants of these wanderers were aware that the Lenape had lived in Sheyichbi for a long, long time.

What we know of the Lenape comes from the work of modern archaeologists and from the writings of early European colonists. Fortunately, there is a sizable body of colonial literature that provides highly detailed descriptions of the Lenape during the two centuries prior to the American Revolution. Unfortunately, much of this literature was written by Europeans who often misunderstood and disliked these Indians.

Sheyichbi was a land teeming with wildlife when the Europeans first came. There were deer, beaver, rabbits, turkey, grouse, bear, and wildcats. The rivers and brooks abounded with fish, and overhead flew thick swarms of game birds. "The quantity of fowl is so great as can hardly be believed," wrote one early sea captain after sailing up the Delaware. "We took at one time 48 partridge together, as they crossed the river, chased by wild hawks." The game was so plentiful that "nothing is wanted but good marksmen with powder and shot," an early colonist wrote. Another said the Lenape were such skillful farmers that they often had surplus foodstuffs to sell to the whites: corn, beans, peaches, watermelons, chestnuts, walnuts, plums, grapes, and wild hops.

Moreover, the bays were rich in oyster beds; whales, if only small ones, made their way into the New York and Delaware bays, and the Indians appear to have hunted them. The rivers and streams yielded catfish, sturgeon, shad, pike, perch, haddock, and turtles. The Lenape "obtain fish of all kinds," one colonist said. In short, Sheyichbi was a bountiful land.

The Lenape (pronounced Len-ah-pay) were a healthy people, "slender and straight as a candle," according to Peter Lindestrom, a colonist in New Sweden on the Delaware River. A Dutchman named Isaack de Rasiere, one of the original European settlers on Manhattan, noted that Lenape men

In this 1702 engraving, Swedish artist Thomas Campanius Holm depicted a friendly exchange between local Indians and traders in New Sweden, on the Delaware River. Holm, who never visited North America, based his fanciful image-- including palm trees--upon descriptions written by his grandfather, who had lived in New Sweden in the 1640s.

generally were "rather tall, well-proportioned in the limbs." Lenape women, according to de Rasiere, were "fine looking, of middle stature, well-proportioned and with finely cut features, with long and black hair, and black eyes set off with fine clothing." Henry Hudson reported the natives were "swarthy." Two other early writers described their complexion as "brownish," and de Rasiere, possibly because he was surprised by the fact, reported that the women "are of the same color as the men." Early writers reported that during warm

5

Jennie Bobb and her daughter, Nellie Longhat (both Delaware), Oklahoma, 1915.

weather, Lenape men and women alike wore little clothing. "They walk naked with only a piece of cloth ... tied around their hips," wrote Johann Printz, a Delaware River colonist. De Rasiere said that "in the wintertime they usually wear a dressed deerskin; some have a bear's skin about the body; some a coat of scales; some a covering made of turkey feathers."

Lenape men never wore beards or moustaches. Indeed, they disliked facial hair so much that when they noticed new whiskers, the men "always pull and pluck out the hair with the roots so that it never gets to grow, but they look smooth on the chin as women," Lindestrom said.

Lindestrom, who provided highly detailed physical descriptions of these Indians, reported that the men used sharp, flint utensils to shave their heads, "allowing tufts to remain here and there, and the bare places they color with red paint." Lindestrom said that men often wore long locks of hair "at the ears which they allow to hang uncut." Lenape women, he wrote "braid their hair in four locks which they allow to hang down the back, or they tie it up in a square pouch on the back."

When Henry Hudson's *Half Moon* first encountered the Lenape, one sailor wrote that some Indians wore "mantles of feathers," and Lindestrom later recorded that "on their heads, they have sitting long and large painted bird feathers."

These Indians also "paint themselves ... in the face with all sorts of colors so that they look inexpressibly horrible," wrote Lindestrom. Printz said the Indian's facial paint made them "terribly ugly." Lindestrom recorded that Lenape and other Indians occasionally cut themselves all over their bodies, then rubbed special ointments into the wounds so that "blue streaks" remained when the wounds healed. This made "the savages appear entirely striped and streaky."

In addition to paint and feathers, the Lenape loved to decorate themselves with wampum fashioned chiefly from seashells, which they called "seewan." "Around their necks they have strung much money, hanging down like a lot of chains on their breasts," Lindestrom said. "Around the head, over the forehead, they bind a belt of money, the width of a hand, and around their waists they have tied a broad belt of money ..., from which their pieces of cloth hang which some of them use to cover themselves." Some natives also used wampum and ribbons to braid their hair, and some even employed it, along with brass and tin, to fashion earrings.

Apparently to add luster to their bodies and hair, these Indians regularly smeared themselves with bear grease, a habit "which makes them smell very rankly," one Dutchman said.

The Lenape lived in small villages situated on hillsides overlooking rivers and creeks. Extensive cornfields, tended chiefly by women and girls, were located nearby. Villages could be as small as three or four families or large enough to have two hundred or three hundred inhabitants. Rarely fortified—and then only by crude log stockades—the villages were mainly sprawling clusters of windowless bark huts. Politically, each village was largely autonomous, ruled, or rather presided over, by a council of elders who appear to have governed by consensus instead of by decree. Though linked by geography, language, customs, and religious beliefs, these villages never constituted formal subdivisions of a larger Lenape state or political entity. The first whites, accustomed to European kings who lorded over huge, well-defined territories, were surprised to find the Lenape culture governed by a multitude of chiefs, each autonomously responsible for precise but small geographic areas. While the Lenape regarded themselves as a single people, known as the Lenni Lenape, this was not expressed geographically. Lenape living along New Jersey's Raritan River considered themselves primarily as Raritan Indians. Lenape living on the Rancocas Creek in the Delaware River Valley called themselves Rancock. There were an

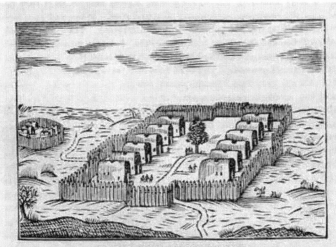

DELAWARE INDIAN FORT.
[From Campanius' "New Sweden."]

estimated eight thousand to twelve thousand Lenape living in a multitude of communities throughout New Jersey, southeastern New York, eastern Pennsylvania, and Delaware when the Europeans first came.

These people had developed a late-Stone-Age culture and had just the beginnings of a knowledge of metals, but virtually all of their tools were fashioned from stone, bone, shell, and wood. Their knowledge of agriculture was so highly developed that their diet was based on foodstuffs produced in their farms and orchards. Although hunting and fishing were essential to their survival, these Indians lived in fixed farming towns rather than in hunting bands that roved in search of game.

While the Indian men were responsible for hunting, fishing, making tools, and clearing fields, the women farmed. Early writers reported:

"Lying in a heap, a whole hill of watermelons, which were as large as pumpkins."

9

"When the maize (corn) is grown two or three feet high, they stick the beans in the ground alongside of the maize-stalks, which serve instead of poles ... for beans to grow on."

Maize "is a grain to which much labor must be given, with weeding and earthing up, or it does not thrive. And to this, the women must attend very closely."

In New Netherlands in 1679, two Europeans were traveling through the woods when they "heard a noise of pounding, like thrashing." Investigating, they found "an old Indian woman busily employed beating Turkish beans out of the pods by means of a stick, which she did with astonishing force and dexterity. Gerrit inquired of her in the Indian Language ... how old she was, and she answered eighty years."

In addition to corn, beans, and watermelons, the Lenape grew pumpkins and squash. Their orchards yielded apples, peaches, and plums. Wild vines produced grapes and berries, and forest trees yielded walnuts, chestnuts, and hazel nuts.

Farming was not a year-round pursuit. The women were finished with the harvest by the time the climate turned cold in autumn, and went "to go with their husbands and children in October to hunt deer, leaving at home with their maize the old people who cannot follow," wrote de Rasiere. "In December they return home, and the flesh which they have not been able to eat while fresh, they smoke on the way, and bring it back with them. They come home fat as moles."

Deer hunting was often a team effort. Sometimes a hundred Indians went into the forest, spaced short distances apart, and, in holding flat thighbones in the hand, beat them with a stick and so drive the creatures before them to the river," reported David de Vries, a Dutch adventurer. As the drive ended, the drivers shot arrows at deer reluctant to go into the river; while deer attempting to escape by swimming away met waiting "savages (who) lie in their canoes with lassos" to rope and strangle them.

Besides deer, hunters pursued elks, rabbits, "foxes in abundance, multitudes of wolves, wild cats, squirrels ... beaver in great numbers, minks, otters, polecats (skunks), bears and many kinds of fur bearing animals which I cannot name or think of," said de Vries. Game birds—turkey, geese, and grouse, to name a few—were also plentiful. Lenape hunters, armed chiefly with bows and other Stone-Age weapons, impressed early colonists as competent marksmen. They were "good and quick shots with their arrows," one colonist wrote.

Native fisherman employed nets, spears and arrows to catch and harpoon fish. Lindestrom describes seeing Lenape men catch "fish of all kinds" by constructing rock walls across most of a brook, "leaving only a little opening or entrance for the fish." This was a trap: "When the river rises and the water is highest, they close up the opening. But when the water is run out and the ebb is lowest, then the fish remains behind in the low water where they either catch them with their hands" or shoot them with arrows. Other writers reported seeing Indians fishing with nets from canoes. Lenape canoes were usually burned out logs, and Lindestrom reported the Lenape even made ocean-going crafts by joining two or more dugout canoes as pontoons. Other Europeans said some Lenape vessels were large enough to carry twenty or more people.

The Day Mannitto
Came to Visit

1609

Before the advent of the Europeans, the Lenape were considerably more than the "devil-worshippers" that many Europeans perceived them to be, and, in fact, appear to have been deeply religious people. The Europeans decided many of their customs and traits were "so inclined to freedom that they cannot by any means be brought to work," Isaack de Rasiere wrote, disparagingly adding, "they are very much addicted to promiscuous intercourse." They also like to gamble. As de Rasiere said, "They are very fond of a game they call Seneca, played with some round rushes which they understand how to shuffle as though they were playing with cards. And they win from each other all that they possess, even to the lappet with which they cover their private parts."

Peter Lindestrom said "they know nothing of taxation" and were "so simple that they ... do not imagine that anything could pass from a man's tongue without coming from the heart."

Henry Hudson's *Half Moon*, in its 1609 voyage along the North American coast, was not the first European ship to appear at Sheyichbi. An Italian explorer, Giovanni da Verrazano, had sailed into New York Bay some eighty years earlier, but had sailed away again without stopping. Moreover, it is known that numerous European ships, their skippers eager to trade for furs with the Indians, had been working the Eastern Seaboard since the 1580s. But these navigators, if indeed they ever encountered the Lenape, left few if any records. At least none survive. The history of the Lenape, then, begins with a skimpy

Giovanni de Verrazano

passage in a chronicle of Verrazano's voyage, and, more fully, with the longer and more descriptive accounts written by Hudson and others on the *Half Moon.*

Verrazano in 1524 said that as his ship sailed into the Hudson, the Lenape had "thirty or more of their small boats, from one shore to the other, filled with multitudes who came to see us. They came towards us with evident delight, raising shouts of admiration and showing us where we could land most securely." The Indians were "dressed out in the feather of birds of various colors."

13

Henry Hudson appears relatively late in the annals of European discovery, questing for a fabled Northwest Passage across North America to Japan and China. Other sea captains had already done considerable exploring by 1609, the year Hudson came into the river that bears his name. The Spanish conquistadors had been strengthening their hold on Central and South America for nearly a century. Hernán Cortez had already conquered Mexico, and Francisco Pizzarro had taken Peru. For nearly half a century the Spanish had had a settlement at Fort Augustine in Florida. Three attempts by the English to plant colonies north of Florida had already failed. Disheartened members of one of Sir Walter Raleigh's two Roanoke Island colonies, both begun in 1585, returned to England within a year. Members of the second venture, the famed "Lost Colony of Roanoke," stayed on, but had vanished by the time English ships returned to the island in 1590. Englishmen sent to Maine by the Plymouth Company in 1607 found life too rugged on the Kennebec River. After less than a year, these colonists also returned to England.

The Jamestown colony, planted by the London Company in 1607, was surviving rather than prospering in southern "Virginia," a name then applied to a vast region stretching from Florida to Maine. On the Saint Lawrence River in Canada, Samuel de Champlain had founded Quebec City in 1608. There were, then, only three European toeholds in North America—the Spanish settlement at St. Augustine, the English one at Jamestown, and the French outpost at Quebec—as Hudson, an Englishman employed by Holland, explored the Atlantic seaboard in 1609. The navigator was aided, according to a member of his crew, Emanuel van Meteren, with "letters and maps which a certain Captain Smith had sent him from Virginia." A soldier and adventurer, John Smith was one of the founders of Jamestown.

Hudson had left Europe in March 1609, making his third quest for the Cathay passage. But he sailed

The Halve Maen (Half Moon) in the Hudson River

so far north that territory he had hoped to penetrate was too choked with ice for his ship to maneuver, so he sailed south along the North Atlantic coast, then gradually began working northward again, exploring the major coastal rivers that he encountered. Hudson sighted the mouth of the shoal-filled Delaware Bay, but did not probe it, opting instead to sail north along New Jersey with its "white sand shore." In early September he rounded Sandy Hook, a long, low stretch of sand that jabs into the sea, dividing the Atlantic and the southeastern edge of the New York harbor.

The *Half Moon* anchored at Sandy Hook, and Hudson sent sailors ashore to fish. It was here that "the people of the country came aboard of us, seeming very glad of our coming," crewman Robert Juet recorded in his diary for September 4. These were undoubtedly Lenape, and this was their earliest known physical contact with Europeans. Juet wrote that they "brought green tobacco" and swapped it for "knives and beads. ... They have yellow copper. They desire clothes and are very civil. They have great stores of maize, or Indian corn, whereof they make good bread."

As peaceful as this first encounter was, a series of events began two days later that prompted Juet's colleague, van Meteren, to characterize the Lenape and other natives along the lower Hudson River as "a strong and warlike people."

By September 6, the *Half Moon* had sailed north into the bay toward the Hudson River, and Hudson sent five sailors to explore upriver in a long boat. For protection, the party was armed with primitive muskets. These firearms were so awkward to use they could be discharged only when a burning fabric, or match, was placed on the firing chambers to ignite the gunpowder. This special fire was kept burning in a separate container known as a match box, ever ready for when the explorers might need their muskets.

Hudson's sailors had completed their assignment and were returning to the *Half Moon* when "they were set upon by two (Indian) canoes, the one having twelve, the other fourteen men. The night came on, and it began to rain, so that their match went out, and they had one man slain in the fight, which was John Colman with an arrow shot into his throat, and two more were hurt," Juet reported. The sailors managed to escape but "it grew so dark that they could not find the ship that night but labored to and fro on their oars."

Unperturbed, Hudson had Colman's body buried ashore, then continued exploring the harbor. The next day he permitted a party of Indians to board the *Half Moon* to trade, and Juet noted they "offered us no violence."

On September 9, "a fair day," the *Half Moon* was menaced by "two great canoes ... full of men." Ostensibly, the Indians had come to trade, but Juet noted they were armed. The crew suspected their announced desire to trade was a ruse, so "we took two of them ... and put red coats on them and would not suffer the others to come near us." The party left, but Hudson kept his two hostages, finally releasing one when another canoe approached the ship. The second hostage "leapt overboard" and escaped. The *Half Moon* tarried in the harbor for two more days, and on the last day "the people of the country came aboard of us, making show of love and gave us tobacco and Indian wheat (apparently corn) ... but we durst not trust them," Juet wrote.

Satisfied that the river was deep enough to navigate and large enough to be the eastern end of the fabled Northwest Passage, Hudson on September 12 began sailing upriver to determine if this actually might be the route. As the ship entered the river, a fleet of twenty-eight canoes "full of men, women and children" approached, but the Europeans feared they came "to betray us ... and suffered none of them to come aboard." Hudson purchased some oysters and beans from this floating market then ordered the ship to proceed upstream.

For ten more days Hudson sailed upriver, but at last the river became too shallow for further navigation, and on September 23, after deciding that the river was not the passage he sought, Hudson reversed course and began descending the river.

The Indians along the upper Hudson, possibly Mohicans, had proved friendlier and much less treacherous than the downriver Indians. As the *Half Moon* returned to the river's lower reaches, the Indians again proved troublesome. The afternoon of October 1, wrote Juet, "one canoe kept hanging under our stern with one man in it ... who got up by our rudder to the cabin window and stole out my pillow and two shirts." Annoyed by the theft, "our master's mate shot at him and struck him on the breast and killed him." Juet's journal indicates that several other canoes had joined in dogging the *Half Moon*, and Juet reported their occupants panicked when the musket was fired. "The rest fled away," he wrote, "some in their boats, and some leapt out of them into the water. We manned our boat, and got our things again. Then one of them that swam got hold of our boat, thinking to overthrow (overturn) it, but our cook took a sword and cut off one of his hands, and he was drowned."

The *Half Moon* had carried the moment, but the ruckus prompted by the incident provoked an Indian attack the next day. "Two canoes full of men with their bows and arrows shot at us from our stern ... We discharged six muskets and killed two or three of them. Then above a hundred of them came to a point of land to shoot at us. There I shot (a small cannon called) a Falcon at them and killed two or three. The rest fled into the woods." Suddenly, the sailors saw "another canoe with nine or ten men, which came to meet us. So I shot at it also ... and shot it through and killed one of them. Then our men with their muskets killed three or four more of them. So they went their way."

Hudson at last was clear from all danger and three days later set sail for England.

By chance, the Indians' version of Hudson's Hudson River exploits has survived. The Lenape created an oral tradition that described the navigator's sudden arrival in their country and passed it along to their descendants. Some 150 years later, as the Delaware Indians, descendants of the Lenni Lenape, passed through central Pennsylvania in the 1700s and headed west to Ohio and Indiana, they took along a tribal memory of the time their ancestors first met European navigators.

The Rev. John Heckewelder, a Moravian missionary who spoke the Delaware language and lived with the Indians for many years, recorded a detailed version of the native legend that told of the first European ship to sail into New York Bay. Writing in his 1818 book *History, Manners and Customs of the Indian Nations Who Once Inhabited Pennsylvania*, the missionary said that he obtained the account "from the mouth of an intelligent Delaware Indian " and that it "may be considered as a correct account of the tradition existing among them of this momentous event." While probably considerably less accurate than

John Heckewelder

Juet's journal in terms of specific facts and details, the tradition nevertheless contains some details corroborated by Juet and seems to provide an authentic statement of the awe and curiosity the Lenape felt when Hudson's *Half Moon* suddenly appeared in their homeland.

As the Indian related the account to Heckewelder:

The Lenape had dwelled in their land for a long time. They had prospered. Their villages and farms were everywhere. Their forests and fields abounded in game; the fish were plentiful in their rivers and streams.

One day at dawn, some Lenape fishermen had paddled their canoes into the bay. They had been fishing for several hours when someone spotted something far out at sea, something that was little larger than a speck. The Indians noticed that it was dark on the bottom and light on the top, and as they watched, they realized that whatever it was appeared to be remarkably large. This realization excited the fishermen, and they stopped fishing to watch the mysterious object, which was still far away on the eastern horizon. Half an hour passed, and the thing had come closer. The Indians realized it was obviously quite large, and now they hurried ashore and summoned their neighbors. They were mystified. "What is it?" they asked. "What do you think it is?"

None of them had ever seen a European sailing ship, and, of course, no one knew it was the double-masted *Half Moon*, sails unfurled. They were curious and launched perhaps ten canoes to paddle into the bay for a closer look. By this time, the ship had come considerably nearer, but not near enough for the Lenape to determine what it was. Some thought it was an uncommonly large fish, but others scoffed at this and argued it was a huge house floating on the sea. Unable to agree, they stayed in the bay, watching, arguing, and growing increasingly apprehensive. The ship, meanwhile, sailed closer, and as the Indians became aware that it was moving steadily towards land, began to believe either it itself was alive or had life within it. Alarmed and overwhelmed, they finally agreed that whatever it was could be hostile and decided the time had come to alert the other Lenape, if only to put them on their guard.

Four canoes were sent to shore to warn the villages along the bay and to summon as many warriors as possible to join the six canoes standing watch in the bay. A commotion resulted in the bay towns, and soon there were thirty canoes filled with armed men in the bay. It was late morning by this time, and the *Half Moon* had come quite close. The Indians agreed now that it was not a fish or animal, but apparently was a strange house that for some reason was definitely, perhaps deliberately, moving up the bay toward the river. But if it was a house, whose house was it? There was considerable arguing over this among both the warriors in the canoes and the hundreds of Indians watching from shore. Many concluded that the house was Mannitto's, and that He was coming to Sheyichbi to visit His people. Obviously, this was what was happening. Ashore and meeting in emergency council, the Lenape chiefs were anxiously attempting to deal with the situation. Obviously, this was Mannitto arriving, but how should they receive him? They ordered a large quantity of meat gathered for a sacrifice, instructed the women to prepare the best victuals for a feast, and told the conjurers and medicine men to determine what this unexpected visit could signify and what its results or consequences could be. The religious leaders and others were bringing out their idols and images and putting them in good order. Plans were under way for a grand dance intended to please Mannitto, but also to appease him if, for some unperceived reason, he might be angry with them. Tremendous confusion, not yet panicky, was developing up and down the land, a strong and frenzied mixture of hope and fear. No one knew precisely what to do or how to interpret the day's strange occurrence. Suddenly, someone started dancing, and just as suddenly, hundreds of other Indians joined in. From all along the shore, and on the islands, came the sounds of fervid chanting and singing, the beating of drums and shaking of turtle shell rattles.

In the villages runners arrived from the bay with news that this strange thing actually was a floating dwelling crowded with living beings. These runners were certain that one of them was Mannitto and that He was bringing them a new kind of animal for game, one He had not given them before. Then other runners came, declaring the house contained humans, but humans who dressed differently than the Indians and whose skin was not brown. One of these people, the later messengers said, was dressed entirely in red, and

Lenni Lenape shaman

He surely must be Mannitto. This news sparked a general panic along the shore, for the house had now entered the river and was rapidly approaching land.

Frightened, many Indians ran into the woods, but others, though equally distraught, stayed at the shore if only to avoid offending the visitors. The house neared land, and its occupants—whoever, whatever they were—shouted ashore in a language the Lenape could not understand. Nevertheless, the Indians shouted back. The Great House drew closer and closer, but stopped a few hundred yards off and lowered a large canoe into the water. This canoe, carrying the red-garbed Mannitto and several others, headed directly for shore. The canoe landed; Mannitto stepped out and walked on the land. Some attendants came with him, but others stayed with the boat, clearly to guard it.

The chiefs and wise men stood nearby, and as Mannitto and His companions approached, the Indian leaders formed a large circle. The Lenape stared at the stranger who saluted with a friendly gesture. Still staring, the Lenape returned the salute. They were awed: He had approached them; at last, had come among their midst. They continued standing in the circle, feeling profoundly honored by this strange being. But lost in admiration and wonder, for a while all they did was stare at him. "Look at him," they thought. "His dress! His friendly manner! Look at his magnificent appearance! His red coat all glittering with gold lace!"

"Surely," they whispered to each other, "This must be the Great Mannitto!" But they also asked, "Why is his skin white?"

"The chiefs and wise men form a large circle to greet the newcomer in a formal council. The man in red approaches them, accompanied by two others. "He salutes them with a friendly countenance and they return the salute ... They are lost in admiration; the dress, the manners, the whole appearance of the unknown strangers is to them a subject of wonder." But the natives are especially impressed with the one "who wore the red coat, all glittering with gold lace. ..." One of Mannitto's companions produces a large, gourd-like bottle and a small glass or cup. "An unknown substance is poured out ... and handed to the supposed Mannitto. He drinks—has the glass filled again and hands it to the chief standing next to him." The Indian takes the glass and sniffs the contents. Instead of taking a sip, he passes the glass to the next chief, who smells the beverage but, declining to drink any, hands the glass to the next chief. The glass is passed all the way around the circle and "is upon the point of being returned to the red-clothed Mannitto when one of the Indians, a brave man and a great warrior, suddenly jumps up and harangues the assembly on the impropriety of returning the cup with its contents. It was handed to them, says he, by the Mannitto that they should drink out of it, as he himself had done. To follow his example would be pleasing to him, but to return what he had given them might provoke his wrath and bring destruction on them."

This Indian announced that he himself would drink the beverage and proclaimed that "it was better for one man to die than that a whole nation should be destroyed." The man took the glass from the chief holding it, bid farewell to everybody, and courageously downed the entire drink. Everyone watched, and "he soon began to stagger and at last fell prostrate on the ground. ... His companions now bemoan his fate. ... He wakes again, jumps up and declares that he has enjoyed the most delicious sensations. ... He asks for more, his wish is granted; the whole assembly then imitate him, and all become intoxicated."

Susquehannocks Meet Captain John Smith

1608

Three ships—the *Susan Constant*, the *God-Speed*, and the *Discovery*— sailed from Blackwell, England, in mid-December 1606, bound for North America. They carried 120 would-be colonists, or planters, who intended to plant the English colony of Virginia.

Most of these passengers styled themselves as gentlemen, but one most notably did not. He was Captain John Smith, a vigorous young man of about twenty-six or twenty-seven who had already had a colorful career in Europe as a soldier of fortune. Smith had fought against the Turks in 1601, and had traveled through the Netherlands, France, Italy, Austria, and Hungary. His military abilities positioned Smith to make a major contribution to the endeavor, but Smith had difficulty in getting along with other members of the expedition. As Charles Dudley Warner reported in his 1881 book, "Captain John Smith," during the Atlantic crossing, some of the expedition's leaders began to suspect that Smith planned to seize control of the colony after the convoy reached its destination.

Quoting from Smith's 1624 book, *The General Historie of Virginia, New England and the Summer Isles*, Warner said that Smith "was restrained as a prisoner upon the scandalous suggestion of some of the chiefs ... who fancied he intended to usurp the government, murder the Council, and make himself King, that his confederates were dispersed in all three ships, and that divers (many) of his confederates ... would affirm it."

The Arrival of the Settlers at Jamestown on May 13, 1607. English Merchantmen of the size and date of the Godspeed, Susan Constant, and the "pinnessee" Discovery maneuvering for anchorage off Jamestown Island 1607.

The convoy finally approached the mouth of the Chesapeake Bay in late April 1607, with Smith arriving as a prisoner. The ships sailed into the bay, and the Englishmen bestowed names on the land formations that bordered the bay. "The cape on the south side is called Cape Henry in honor of our most noble prince," John Smith said later. Henry was the Prince of Wales. "The north cape," Smith continued, "is called Cape Charles in honor of the worthy Duke of York." In time, the duke ascended the English throne as King Charles I.

Throughout his career, Smith demonstrated considerable skill in extricating himself from difficult situations. During the next sixteen months, the adventurer progressed from prisoner to president of the colony. As it turned out, events in Jamestown as well as Smith's own exploits were important factors in his September 1608 selection as head of the settlement.

Captain John Smith and eleven other Europeans explored the Chesapeake Bay and its tributaries in a barge that hardly weighed two tons. Only two or three members of the expedition had any experience in sailing. Most of them were, in Smith's word, "gentlemen" generally unfamiliar with "toil and labor" and who lacked the specific skills needed on the voyage "to trim their sails, use their oars or any business belonging to the barge." But necessity as well as prompting and prodding by the captain saw them quickly learn to do the work.

Setting out from Jamestown on the James River, their provisions consisted "of nothing but a little meal or oatmeal and water." They survived because Indians they met along the way gave or sold food to them, and the explorers also caught "plenty of fish that they found in all places."

In late summer of 1608 Smith's crew was slowly rowing the barge across the Chesapeake when a fleet of Massawomeck canoes suddenly appeared. The Indians came in seven or eight canoes, and the Englishmen saw that these were warriors preparing to assault the boat. The Massawomecks were still a good distance away, and Smith faced a big challenge, for most of his men were sick, apparently suffering from malaria. Indeed, only Smith and four others were well enough to stand. If the warriors, who were closing in fast, realized that defending the barge would be all but impossible. The captain opted for a ruse, and directed the men who were well to carry their ill comrades under the boat's tarpaulin. Then "we put their hats upon sticks by the barge side to make us seem many," Smith said. Misled by this trick, the warriors put into shore rather than attempt an attack, "and there stayed, staring at the sailing of our barge til we anchored right against them."

The colonists befriended the natives, and when Smith gave bells to the first two Indians that boarded the barge, the other warriors also came aboard. The Massawomecks were so pleased and impressed that they gave Smith an assortment of weapons as gifts— bows, arrows, and clubs. "We understood them nothing at all but by signs, whereby they signified ... they had been at war with the Tockwoghs ... which

Captain John Smith

they confirmed by showing their green (fresh) wounds," Smith reported.

The next day, the colonists explored the Tockwogh River. A fleet of Indian canoes soon surrounded them, and the warriors were all armed. But these Tockwoghs decided to be friendly. When they asked through an interpreter why the Europeans had Massawomeck weapons, Smith told them that his men had taken them after defeating the Massawomeck warriors in a fight.

The Indians were sufficiently impressed to invite Smith's crew to their town, which was surrounded by a log palisade. Inside the wall they had erected scaffold-like mounts and had used broad pieces of tree bark to cover their houses. Men, women, and children greeted the Englishmen and entertained them kindly "with dances, songs, fruits, fish, fur and what they had," Smith said. The Virginians were surprised to see that Tockwoghs had pieces of iron and brass as well as many hatchets and knives made of metal. The Tockwoghs said that they had obtained these implements from the Susquehannocks.

Smith persuaded the Tockwoghs to send messengers to the Susquehannocks, who lived two days' travel up the Susquehanna River, and invite them to come down to the Chesapeake to meet the Virginians. Several days later, "60 of these giant-like people came down with presents of venison, tobacco pipes, baskets, targets, bows and arrows," Smith said. Five of their chiefs "came boldly aboard us to cross the bay for Tockwogh, leaving their men and canoes, the wind being so violent that they durst not pass."

As Smith described the encounter afterwards: He and his crew sailed as far up the Chesapeake as they could until they came to "the end of the bay where it is six or seven miles in breadth." He found several rivers there, including "one that commeth due north, three or four days' journey from the head of the bay, and falls from rocks and mountains. Upon this river inhabit a people called Susquehannock. ... They can make near 600 able and mighty men."

"Sixty of these Susquehannocks came to the discoverers with skins, bows, arrows, targets, beads, swords and tobacco pipes for presents. ... Those are the most strange people of all those countries, both in language and attire." These Indians wore clothing fashioned from the skins of bears and wolves. One man had a shirt made from a bearskin with the head still attached. The native wore the garment in such a way that the "man's neck goes through the skin's neck

..., the nose and teeth hanging down his breast," Smith wrote. "The ears of the bear (were) fastened to his shoulders."

Another Susquehannock sported a tobacco pipe "three quarters of a yard long, prettily carved with a bird" at one end. Others had similar pipes that contained carvings of bears or deer. The ends of these pipes were sufficiently sturdy to serve as clubs that could "beat out the brains of a man," Smith said.

These warriors appeared friendly, and Smith reported that they possessed "an honest and simple disposition." Five of their chiefs came aboard the barge and crossed the bay on it, he said. The chief that Smith regarded as the most powerful was a tall, well-proportioned man. He wore his hair long on one side, and cropped close on the other, "with a ridge over his crown, like a cock's comb."

The arrows belonging to this chief were forty-five inches long, and "headed with flints or splinters of stone, in form like a heart, an inch broad and an inch and a half or more long," Smith said. He kept them in a quiver made from a wolf skin, which he wore on his back. He carried "his bow in one hand, and his club in the other," he reported.

Through interpreters, the Susquehannocks told Smith that they lived in towns protected by palisade walls as a defense against the Iroquois who lived in the north. The Susquehannocks said that their towns were located two days' travel above the bay, and a frustrated Smith realized that the river was too shallow for his boat to navigate.

At one point during the Susquehannocks' visit, "they were long busied with consultation till they had contrived their business; then they began in most passionate manner to hold up their hands to the sun with a most fearful song," Smith said. During the singing, several of the Susquehannocks suddenly embraced the captain. "He rebuked them, yet they proceeded till their song was finished ... That ended, with a great painted bear's skin they covered our

Tockwogh village

captain. Then one ready with a chain of white beads, weighing at least six or seven pound(s), hung it about his neck. The others had 18 mantles (covers) made of divers (diverse) sorts of skins sewed together. All these, with many other toys, they laid at his feet, stroking their ceremonious hands about his neck."

At this point the Susquehannocks asked Smith "to be their governor, promising their aids, victuals, or what they had to be his, if he would stay with them to defend and revenge them of the Massawomecks." But the explorer declined the honor. When the Jamestown barge left the Tockwogh town, the Susquehannocks expressed "much sorrowing for our departure, yet we promised the next year again to visit them. Many descriptions and discourses they made us of ... other people, signifying they inhabit the river of Canada, and from the French ... have their hatchets, and ... like tools by trade."

Etienne Brule Explores the Susquehanna

1615

Etienne Brule *(Ay-tee-en Bru-lay)* was born in France around 1592, sailed to Canada as a teenaged boy in 1608, and in 1610 was sent to live with the Huron Indians on the Great Lakes.

Many historians credit Brule, who became a frontier interpreter, with being the first European to travel the length of the Susquehanna River. Details of this feat remain vague and even murky. What little we know was recorded by none other than Samuel de Champlain, the explorer and founder of New France. Not only did Etienne Brule know Champlain, but he appears to have been, first, his ward, if only informally, and, later, his interpreter.

Champlain founded Quebec in July 1608, and Brule, then a boy of about sixteen, appears to have been one of its first residents. Champlain himself is the source of this. Indeed, Champlain reports that by the summer of 1610, this boy "had already spent two winters at Quebec."

Champlain's journals of his travels to and in Canada, the Jesuit Relations, and Brother Gabriel Sagard's book of his 1624 missionary work among the Hurons in Canada all provide sketchy details of the life of Etienne Brule, an obscure but vigorous explorer who was one of the first Europeans to see the Great Lakes. Although he served Champlain and the French priests as an interpreter, he seems to have adapted quite thoroughly to life among the Indians.

Few facts are known about Etienne Brule, and it is difficult to sketch more than an outline of his life; nonetheless, two people who knew him—Samuel de

Etienne Brule

Champlain and Brother Sagard—left such rich records of New France, Canada, the Indians, and the French colonists, that it is possible to gain a good sense of the times in which Brule lived. Sagard and Champlain are the primary sources.

1608

Samuel de Champlain arrived in North America in mid-1608, the lieutenant of a friend of King Henry of France. The friend had a royally granted monopoly "to trade in peltry and other merchandise for the period of one year only" in New France. The king had also directed his friend, the Sieur de Monts, to establishment a permanent settlement so that "our subjects can go there to trade without hindrance."

The Frenchmen had made landfall in June at a place called Tadoussac near the mouth of the Saguenay, a coastal river. Champlain, finding de Monts recovering from a serious wound, set out in search of a place to build an outpost that could serve both French traders coming from Europe and Native Americans bringing furs to barter for glass beads and tools and weapons made of metal. He sailed up the St. Lawrence, headed for a neck of land that the Algonquin Indians called Quebec, a word that meant "the narrowing of the waters."

"I arrived there on the 3rd of July, when I searched for a place suitable for our settlement, but I could find none more convenient or better situated than the point of Quebec ..., which was covered by nut trees," Champlain wrote. Champlain decided to build the trading post on this spot, and quickly organized his workmen. Some set about felling the trees; others sawed lumber from the logs, and still others constructed a storehouse for the expedition's supplies.

Bizarrely, one of the workers, a locksmith by trade, organized a mutiny among the men. They plotted to strangle Champlain and take control of the post, but the explorer learned of the plan and arrested the conspirators. Champlain and other leaders of the colony decided to send most of the mutineers back to France, but they executed the principal plotter, a man named Jean du Val. According to Champlain, they had du Val strangled, hung, and beheaded, "and his head was put on the end of a pike ... set up in the most conspicuous place on our fort."

Confident that he has suppressed insurrection from within, Champlain subsequently had his workers erect three two-story buildings to provide housing near the storehouse. They fortified the complex, armed its outer defenses with cannon, and dug a moat around it. They also established a number of gardens.

Some colonists also took the time to explore the neighborhood. To their surprise, they found the ruins of a European settlement about two miles up the St. Charles River, which entered the St. Lawrence near Quebec. Champlain described the ruins of "a chimney ... and indications of there having been ditches surrounding their dwelling, which was small. We found, also, large pieces of hewn, worm-eaten timber and some three or four cannon balls." He speculated that this was the site where French navigator Jacques Cartier had wintered while exploring Canada in 1535.

In mid-September, Champlain and many colonists remained at Quebec when the ship that had brought them to America returned to France. A close reading of the explorer's journal shows no other colonists arriving or leaving the outpost after that. Thus, the story of Etienne Brule's life in America clearly begins in 1608, when, whatever his role, he became one of the first residents of Quebec. Two years later, Champlain said that the youngster had spent the winter of 1608-09 in the settlement.

1609

For the fur trade to prosper, the French needed the good will and active cooperation of the Hurons, Algonquins, and other northern tribes that controlled access to the rivers and lakes of Canada. Champlain worked diligently to befriend these Indians, and they

Etienne Brule and Huron warriors at the mouth of the Humber River.

began to press him to take their side in their never-ending war against a tribe that lived to the south of the St. Lawrence. Their enemies were the Iroquois, and they occupied land along a large lake in what is now New York State.

Champlain set out in July, leading a small force that consisted of two French soldiers armed with muskets and a mixture of Algonquins, Montagnais, and Hurons equipped with bows and arrows. "The savages," Champlain said, "made a review of all their followers, finding that there were 24 canoes with 60 men." The Indians and French advanced stealthily, camping and sleeping by day and moving toward the Iroquois settlements by night. It was late in the month when Champlain's force encountered a large party of Iroquois warriors, who knew the invaders had arrived. "They had come to fight," the Frenchman wrote.

Both sides spent the night before the battle in singing and dancing. In the morning, the Iroquois emerged from a barricade of logs, and Champlain noted there were about two hundred of them. They marched toward the Canadian Indians, then stopped and stood in a formation. Three of their chiefs took positions out in front. The French Indians ran toward them, but came to a halt just out of the range of the Iroquois arrows. As this happened, Champlain had remained in the rear of his force, and had watched as his soldiers, each carrying a musket, walked a short distance into the woods. Champlain's Indian allies grew eager for the battle to begin, and they clamored for Champlain to start it. "Our men began to call me with loud cries, and, in order to give me a passageway, they opened in two parts and put me at their head, where I marched some 20 paces in advance of the rest."

The Frenchman advanced to about one hundred feet from the Iroquois, who stared at him. He suspected that the Iroquois had never seen or heard a gun before. "When I saw them making a move to fire at us, I rested my musket against my cheek and aimed directly at one of the three chiefs," he said. Champlain fired and struck two chiefs, knocking them down, and mortally wounded a third Indian. "When our side saw this shot so favorable for them, they began to raise such loud cries that one could not have heard it thunder," Champlain wrote. "Meanwhile, arrows flew on both sides."

As Champlain reloaded, the other French soldiers opened fire, and the sound of their shots prompted the Iroquois to panic. "Seeing their chiefs dead, they lost courage and took flight," he wrote. Though vastly outnumbered, the Indians from Canada pursued their foes, killed a number of them, and captured about a dozen. They looted the Iroquois camp then struck out for Canada.

That night, the victorious Indians decided to torture one of their Iroquois prisoners. Appalled by this episode, Champlain nevertheless recorded many details of the man's torture and death: The Indians built a fire and made firebrands, which they used to burn the captive's entire body. "Sometimes they stopped and threw water on his back. Then they tore out his nails, and applied fire to the extremities of his fingers and private member. Afterwards, they flayed the top of his head, and had a kind of gum poured all hot upon it." Following this, they mutilated his body. "This poor wretch uttered terrible cries, and it excited my pity to see him treated in this manner." Champlain objected and insisted that the Indians allow him to shoot the man in order to end his suffering, but they refused. At length—and only to appease Champlain— they let him kill the Iroquois with a musket shot.

Champlain's allies then committed what he called "another monstrosity." They removed the dead man's heart, cut it into pieces, and forced his brother and several other prisoners, all friends of the executed captive, to eat it. "They took it into their mouths, but would not swallow it," Champlain said. In the end, the Algonquins who guarded these captives let them spit it out. As the expedition made its way north, most of the other prisoners were also tortured and killed.

It was August by the time Champlain returned to French Canada. He noted that some of his Indian allies, the Montagnais, carried the heads of some of these prisoners for hundreds of miles until at last they reached their homes. "On approaching the shore, they each took a stick, to the end of which they hung the heads of their enemies ... The women ... in a state of entire nudity ... jumped into the water and swam to the prows of the canoes to take the heads of their enemies."

Several days later these Indians presented Champlain with "one of these heads ... and also with a pair of arms" to take to France and to show the king. "This, for the sake of gratifying them, I promised to do," Champlain wrote.

Samuel de Champlain

In September the explorer sailed for France after posting fifteen men at the fort at Quebec. One of them, presumably, was a boy named Etienne Brule, who would have been about seventeen.

Incidentally, the explorer named the lake where the battle took place after himself, and we know it today as Lake Champlain.

1610

In June 1610 Champlain and a small number of French soldiers, together with a force of Indian allies, departed Quebec and struck out for the mouth of the River of the Iroquois (the Richelieu River). Four hundred other Indians, including a force of Algonquins, were to meet him there, and they were to

39

attack the Iroquois. But the Algonquins had begun fighting the Iroquois in a forest before Champlain arrived. The Iroquois defended themselves from inside a log barricade, and the Algonquins were unable to dislodge them. Champlain and the other Frenchmen joined the battle as rapidly as they could. "We commenced firing numerous musket-shots through the brush wood, since we could not see them."

From inside their stockade, the Iroquois apparently had a clear view of the French and showered the attackers with arrows. Their shots proved lethal. "I was wounded while firing my first shot ... by an arrow which pierced the end of my ear and entered my neck," Champlain wrote later. "I seized the arrow and tore it from my neck. The end of it was armed by a very sharp stone." Despite the wound, he managed to continue firing his gun. "You could see the arrows fly on all sides thick as hail. The Iroquois were astonished at the noise of our muskets, and especially that the balls penetrated better than their arrows."

As the fighting progressed, the French musketeers advanced to the stockade walls and shot through openings between the palisades. "We scarcely ever missed, firing two or three balls at one shot, resting our muskets most of the time on the side of their barricade," Champlain said. Inside the stockade, the Iroquois became terrified when they saw some of the musket shot kill and wound some of their comrades. "They were so frightened ... that ... they threw themselves on the ground whenever they heard a discharge," Champlain reported.

When the French realized that they would run out of shot before the Iroquois used up their arrows, Champlain convinced his Indians to storm the stockade. Some of the Indians felled large trees, which fell on the palisade walls, breaching them. The French fired "salvos of musketry" into the stockade just before the Algonquins stormed it. Many of the Iroquois died in the attack. Others escaped, but of these, fifteen were later captured.

"The savages," Champlain reported, "scalped the dead, and took the heads as a trophy of victory, according to their custom. ... They attached to sticks in the prows of their canoes the heads and a dead body cut into quarters, to eat in revenge, as they said." They also took the fifteen captives with them and tortured and executed them at various places along the way.

A few days after the battle, an Algonquin war chief, Captain Iroquet, arrived with some eighty men and expressed regret that he had missed the fighting.

Champlain, the French soldiers, the Algonquins, and, presumably, the surviving prisoners all spent several days on an island near the mouth of the River of the Iroquois (the Richelieu). It was here that Champlain did a curious thing. "I had a young lad, who had already spent two winters at Quebec, and who was desirous of going with the Algonquins to learn their language," the explorer said. "Going to Captain Iroquet, who was strongly attached to me, I asked him if he would like to take this boy to his country to spend the winter with him and bring him back in the spring. He promised to do so and treat him like his own son, saying he was greatly pleased with the idea."

Champlain believed that the French interest would benefit if the boy, whom scholars have identified as Etienne Brule, learned the language and culture of the Indians as well as the nature of the country, rivers, and lakes where the Indians lived. Brule, who had been born in France in 1591 or 1592, was about eighteen or nineteen years old. He appears to have had no family members present to watch out for his interests. "We asked him," Champlain wrote in a wily way, "if it was his desire to go, for I did not wish to force him. But he answered the question at once by consenting to the journey with great pleasure."

When the Algonquins expressed concern about the boy's ability to survive when forced to live like an Indian, the French leader had a ready answer. "I replied that the boy would be able to adapt himself without difficulty to their manner of living and usual food and that, if through sickness or the fortunes of war any harm should befall him, this would not interrupt my friendly feelings toward them."

The Algonquins insisted that in exchange Champlain take one of their boys back to France with him, and he quickly agreed. "We parted with many promises of friendship," Champlain said. The explorer sailed for Europe in August and took the Indian boy along.

1611

Champlain set sail for North America in March 1611, but the voyage took several months, and it was mid-May when he reached Quebec. His company included the Indian boy, whom his journal refers to repeatedly as "the savage." In late May, Champlain headed for a great waterfall several days travel from Quebec. He expected to meet the Algonquins there, but the Indians hadn't arrived by the time Champlain got there.

On June 2 "we resolved to send Savignon, our savage, together with another, to meet his countrymen so as to hasten his arrival. They hesitated about going in our canoe, it being a very poor one."

Seven days later, Savignon and his companion returned and reported that they hadn't encountered any other Indians and that they had traveled until their canoe gave out. They added that after passing the fall, "they saw an island, where there was such a quantity of herons that the air was completely filled with them."

It was June 13 when the Algonquin allies finally arrived. There were two hundred Hurons coming by canoe. "We were greatly pleased to see them," Champlain said. "As they were approaching slowly and in order, our men prepared to salute them with a discharge of arquebuses, muskets and small pieces." But the gunfire alarmed them, and "they begged me to assure them that there would be no more firing, saying that the greater part of them had never seen Christians nor heard thunderings of that sort and that they were afraid ..."

Reunited with his people, Savignon told about his traveling to Europe, "commended the treatment I had shown him in France, and the remarkable objects he had seen."

Captain Iroquet had also brought Etienne Brule along. "I also saw my servant, who was dressed in the costume of the savages," Champlain reported. The lad "commended the treatment he had received from them" and "informed me of all he had seen and learned during the winter ..."

Savignon appears to have preferred staying with Champlain to returning to his own people, but Champlain had other ideas. Some days after the Hurons arrived, "I gave some trifles to Savignon, who set out much pleased, giving me to understand that he was about to live a very irksome life in comparison with that he had led in France. He expressed much regret at separation, but I was very glad to be relieved of the care of him."

1615

The summer of September 1615 Champlain traveled to the land of the Hurons and prepared to go to war against the Iroquois. The Hurons were eager to assist him and reported that they had received word "that a certain nation of their allies ... on whom the Iroquois also make war, desired to assist them in this expedition with 500 good men." These Indians were the Susquehannocks, and Champlain wrote that his Huron allies described them as "very warlike. ... They have only three villages, which are in the midst of more than 20 others, on which they make war without assistance from their friends."

In early September the explorer set out with a force of Frenchmen and Indian allies. As the soldiers and warriors progressed, Champlain sent a party to

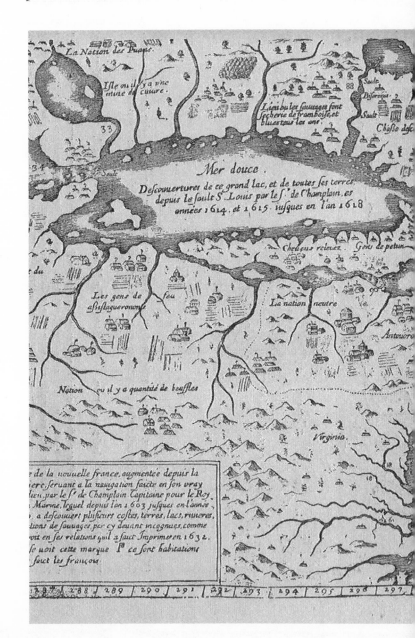

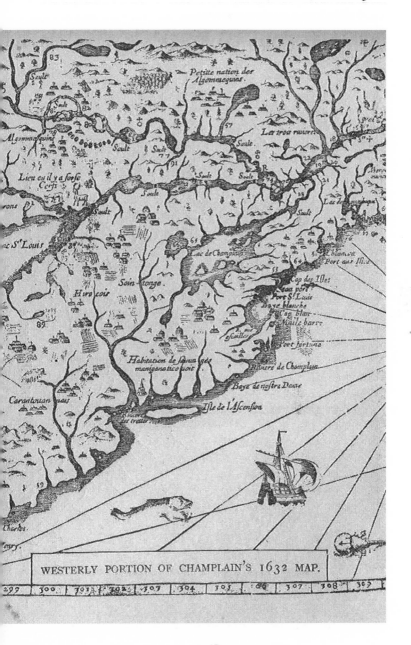

WESTERLY PORTION OF CHAMPLAIN'S 1632 MAP.

summon the Susquehannocks. "It was decided to choose some of the most resolute men ... to go and give notice ... to those who were to assist us with 500 men, that they might join us and that we might appear together before the fort of the enemy."

The Hurons selected twelve capable warriors who would travel in two canoes. It would take a good three days to reach the palisaded towns of these allies, and there would be great danger "since it was necessary to pass through the midst of enemies," Champlain reported. He added that "one of our interpreters ... asked me to permit him to make the journey, which I readily accorded ... as he might in this way see their country and get a knowledge of the people living there."

This interpreter was Etienne Brule, then a young man of about twenty-three. Champlain fully expected to see the interpreter, his Indian escort, and the force of five hundred warriors from the Susquehanna arrive in two to three weeks, but years would pass before interpreter and governor would meet again.

By the ninth of October, Champlain's army reached the Iroquois fort a few miles south of Oneida Lake in central New York. "Their village was enclosed by four good wood palisades, which were made of great pieces of wood, interlaced with each other, with an opening of not more than half a foot between two, and which were 30 feet high, with galleries after the manner of a parapet, which they had furnished with double pieces of wood ..." The town was near a pond, and the Indians had fashioned gutters that provided water at the base of the stockade. They used the water to extinguish any fires that Champlain's men might set on the wall. The French built a tall wooden structure, equipped it with shooting platforms, and placed it near the village wall. Champlain then had some of his soldiers climb the structure and "keep up a constant fire over their palisades and galleries." At first, the Iroquois showered the structure with arrows and stones, but the firepower of the French shooters soon forced the Iroquois to abandon their defensive platforms along the top of the palisade. When they began using their bows and weapons from less strategic positions, they found that their weapons were ineffective against Champlain's firing tower.

As effective as this tactic was, Champlain's Indian allies didn't understand the French style of fighting and wouldn't use large wooden shields that his men had fashioned for their protection against the Iroquois arrows. Instead, "they ... began to scream at their enemies, shooting arrows into the fort, which in my opinion did little harm to the enemy," Champlain said. "In vain did I shout in their ears ... as to the danger to which they exposed themselves by their bad behavior, but on account of the great noise they made they heard nothing."

The day ended with Champlain withdrawing his force, leaving the Iroquois in control of the town. The Hurons were disheartened by Champlain's failure to take the Iroquois, but the French and Hurons decided they would make another attempt when Etienne Brule arrived with the five hundred warriors from the Susquehanna River.

Around the sixteenth of October, the Hurons realized that their allies were probably not coming, so they decided to return to their own country. In preparing to leave, they made "a kind of basket for carrying the wounded, who are put into it crowded up in a heap being bound ... in such a manner that it is impossible for them to move," Champlain wrote. He himself had been shot by Iroquois arrows and was carried off to Canada in a Huron basket. "The pain that I suffered in consequence of the wound in my knee was nothing in comparison with that which I endured while I was carried ... on the back of one of our savages," Champlain recounts.

As events played out, the Susquehannocks accompanying Etienne Brule arrived at the Iroquois town two days after Champlain's army had departed. Finding the French and Hurons gone, the

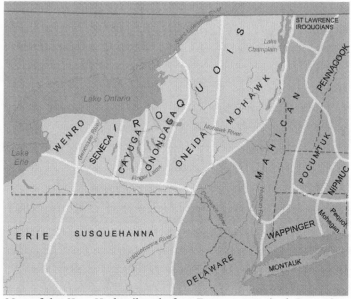

Map of the New York tribes before European arrival: Iroquoian on left and Algonquian on right.

Susquehannocks returned to the lower Susquehanna River. Etienne Brule went with them.

Three years would pass before he again saw Champlain and New France. It was 1618 when Brule finally returned to Canada and gave Champlain a belated report of his adventures.

1618

Champlain left Paris in late March, destined for Canada. Ordinarily, the adventurer sailed from the French port of Honfleur, and this year was no exception. But instead of departing immediately for North America, "we were obliged to make a long stay on account of contrary winds." It was May 24 when Champlain's ship finally departed. The voyage was a speedy one, and "we arrived at Quebec on the 27th of June ..." He inspected the town, then "I visited the cultivated lands, which I found with fine grain. The gardens contained all kinds of plants, cabbages, radishes, lettuce, purslain, sorrel, parsley and other plants, squashes, cucumbers, melons, peas, beans and other vegetables, which were as fine and forward as in France. There were also the vines, which had been transplanted, already well advanced."

Champlain left Quebec in early July, and sailed up the St. Lawrence, bound for a place called Trois Rivieres, where he expected to meet the Hurons and other Indians who had come to trade and to renew their friendship with the French and their governor. In part, the Indians wanted Champlain to tell them "whether I would again assist them, as I had done in the past ..., in their wars with the enemies, by whom they are cruelly harassed and tortured." The governor promised that subject to certain conditions—namely that they bring to justice some Indians who the prior year had murdered two Frenchmen—his soldiers would "assist them and enable them to enjoy ... victory over their enemies."

Champlain's comments pleased the Indians mightily. "Two or three days after my arrival," he wrote, "they proceeded to make merry, dance and celebrate many great banquets in view of the future war in which I was to assist them."

It is at this point in his narrative that Champlain describes his unexpected reunion with Etienne Brule. "Now there was with them," Champlain writes, "a man named Etienne Brule, one of our interpreters, who had been living with them for eight years."

Champlain was now roughly twice the age of Brule. Born around 1567 in France, the Catholic explorer was about fifty-one years old. Brule was about twenty-six.

"I called this man ... and asked him why he had not brought the assistance of the 500 men, and what was the cause of the delay and why he had not rendered me a report," Champlain said.

To Champlain's surprise, the interpreter explained that he and the Indians had indeed set out to summon the Susquehannocks. But they found the trail dangerous, and "since they had to pass through the territories of their enemies ... (they) pursued a more secure route through thick and impenetrable forests, woods and brushy, marshy bogs and unfrequented places and wastes ..." They even encountered some Iroquois, whom they surprised. They killed four men and took two others as prisoners. Brule's party took the captives with them and hurried on to the Susquehannock town, which Champlain referred to as Carantouan.

Instead of rushing to the aid of the Algonquins and their French friends, the Susquehannocks received the messengers "with great affection, a cordial welcome and good cheers," then treated Brule and the members of his escort "with the dances and banquets with which they are accustomed to entertain and honor strangers." Several days passed in what Brule described as "this friendly reception," and then—"after Brule had told them of his mission"—the Susquehannocks met to consider the message. Following due deliberation, they agreed to take part in the fighting, and they began to mobilize their warriors. "These," Brule told Champlain, "were very long in getting ready, although urged by Brule make haste." The interpreter also said that he explained to the Indians "that if they delayed any longer, they would not find us there."

When the Susquehannocks finally arrived at the Iroquois fort, Champlain, the French soldiers, and the Algonquin Indians had already withdrawn. The Susquehannocks returned to their town, Carantouan, and Brule went with them. The interpreter explained to Champlain that he had felt "obliged to stay and spend the rest of the autumn and all of the winter for lack of company and escort home."

Far from letting himself become bored and inactive in the Susquehannock town, Brule said he "busied himself in exploring the country ... and in making a tour along a river that debouches in the direction of

Florida, where there are many powerful and warlike nations, carrying on wars against each other. ... He continued his course along the river as far as the sea and to islands and lands near them. ... Among other things, he observed that the winter was very temperate, that it snowed rarely, and that when it did, the snow was not a foot deep and melted immediately."

Historians have long maintained that the river Brule traveled was the Susquehanna and that he followed first the river and then the Chesapeake Bay to eastern Virginia, where the bay meets the Atlantic Ocean.

Brule told Champlain that Indians along this river "love the French ... but those who know the Dutch complain severely of them since they treated them very roughly." (Henry Hudson and other Dutch explorers had begun penetrating the Delaware and Hudson rivers, and the French rightly regarded them as rivals for the Indian trade.)

Brule related that sometime in the spring of 1616, he set out for Canada, accompanied by half a dozen Susquehannocks. The travelers met an Iroquois war party, and the Frenchman became separated from his Indian companions. He said that he wandered through the forest for several days without eating. He came upon some Iroquois "savages loaded with fish repairing to their village." He called out to them, convinced them that he wasn't hostile, and got them to feed him. They even smoked a pipe and took him to their village "where they entertained him."

But other Iroquois men hated the French, whom they referred to as "men of iron." When they learned Brule was in the town, they took him by force and began torturing him. They tied him up, and "tore out his (finger)nails with their teeth, burnt him with glowing firebrands and tore out his beard, hair by hair ..."

Brule was in the habit of wearing a religious medal, the Agnus Dei, around his neck, and one of the Indians torturing him grabbed it and began tugging on

Agnus Dei, "Lamb of God"

the chain. The Frenchman warned that "if you take it and put me to death ..., you will suddenly die." Just then, the sky darkened, lightning flashed, and thunder rolled. The sudden storm produced "thunders and lightnings so violent and long" that the Indians were terrified. They just left him, and an Indian who had befriended him came over and untied him. The man "took him to his house where he took care of him and treated his wounds. After this, there were no dances, banquets or merry-makings to which Brule was not invited."

In due time, Etienne Brule left the Iroquois and returned to the Huron town where he had lived.

As fabulous as Brule's report may seem, Champlain appears to have accepted it at face value.

"After he had made this recital," the older Frenchman wrote, "I gave him assurance that his services would be recognized ... He took leave of me to return to the savages ... (and) I begged him to continue with them until the next year when I would return with a good number of men ..."

Champlain tarried at Trois Rivieres for about a week. "The trading having been concluded and the savages having taken their leave and departed, we left Trois Rivieres on the 14th of July," Champlain reported. He and his men sailed down the St. Lawrence, and stopped at Quebec. Merchandise that hadn't been traded with the Indians was returned to the storehouse, and Champlain devoted several days to repairing and improving the fortifications at the trading post. He left the settlement on July 26 after promising the Catholic priests, traders, and colonists "that I would return, God assisting, with a good number of families to people the country."

He was back in France by August 28, "the wind having been favorable," he wrote.

Etienne Brule, meanwhile, was deep in North American, living, dressing, speaking, and, quite possibly, thinking like an Algonquin Indian.

1624

Sagard the missionary described in great and gory detail the way that the Hurons tortured their Iroquois captives. With some prisoners, "they ... cut off the three principal fingers which are employed in drawing the bow," then burn them with fire and hot ashes. Other captives were forced to "walk with naked body and feet through a great number of fires kindled for the purpose from one end to the other of a great lodge. ... All the people ranged along the two sides, each holding a burning brand in his hand (and) apply these to their bodies as they pass." Throughout—and despite —the torture, the prisoners chant "a very sad and mournful song." When nearly dead, "the prisoner is taken out of the lodge" and placed on a scaffold erected especially for the occasion. "There his head is cut off. Then his belly is opened, and all the little children are there to get some small fragment of bowel which they hang on the end of a stick and carry ... through the whole town. ... When the body is thus disemboweled and prepared, they cook it in a large kettle and eat it at a feast with jollity and rejoicing ..."

Sagard added, "When the Iroquois or other enemies can catch any of our people, they do the same to them."

1629

Some English adventurers coveted Quebec and managed to recruit Etienne Brule, then a man of about thirty-seven, to guide them up the Saint Lawrence River on a raid. The Englishmen easily took the town. Whatever his motives, Brule's role in the episode cost him many of the friendships he had enjoyed with his countrymen in New France. As for Champlain, he never forgave Brule's act of betrayal, and many French colonists joined the governor in regarding Brule as a traitor.

The taking of Quebec had occurred at a time when England and France were at peace. In the end, the English conquerors of New France were obliged to return the colony back to the French, and Etienne Brule never lived down his treachery.

1633

Brule's final adventure played itself out deep in the country of the Hurons. At a village called Toanache, the Frenchman ran afoul of some Huron chiefs who executed him. As Brother Sagard reported, "Brule was ... condemned to death and eaten by the Hurons."

The slaying of Etienne Brule caused a panic among the Indians, who feared that Champlain would retaliate. Fearing reprisals when news of Brule's death reached the colonial government, they abandoned the village.

Later that year, the Jesuit priest chronicling events in New France noted that on July 28, there arrived in Quebec a fleet of about 140 canoes, "carrying easily 500 Hurons—or 700, as some say—with their merchandise." In coming down from the Great Lakes, the fleet had encountered two tribes along the route who "had tried to dissuade them from visiting the French, saying we would do them a bad turn on account of the death of one Brule, whom they had killed."

But Samuel de Champlain and other French leaders weren't interested in punishing the Indians for murdering Brule. After all, as Louis Amantacha, Champlain's representative, told the Hurons, "He was not looked upon as a Frenchman because he had left his nation and gone over to the service of the English."

Indians Murder Whalers at Cape Henlopen

1631

In 1631 a Dutch commercial entity called the West India Company deposited thirty-two settlers, all men, on Cape Henlopen, Delaware, and instructed them to develop a colony devoted to farming and whaling. The would-be colonists landed with a small herd of horses and cows, as well as the boats, ropes, harpoons, and other equipment needed to catch and process whales, which were plentiful in Delaware Bay.

The colony, which the Dutch called Swannendael, appeared to prosper. The settlers quickly erected a fort and surrounded it with a log palisade. They also took pains to establish peaceful relations with the neighboring Indians.

As the Europeans set about establishing their fishery and farm, all was well—or at least the colonists thought it was. But one day the Indians turned on the Dutchmen, massacred all of them, and killed off all the colony's livestock. Months later, when additional colonists arrived at Swannendael, they found a desolate, fire-charred outpost. No Indians were about. Nor were there any Europeans. As the new arrivals wandered through the ruins of Swannendael plantation, they "found lying here and there the skulls and bones of our people, and the heads of the horses and cows they had brought with them."

Since none of the original colonists had survived the massacre, only Indians were available to tell what had provoked Swannendael's destruction. When Indians eventually arrived to meet the new colonists, they provided a strange explanation: The Swannendael colonists had erected a wood pole near their fort, and

"Landing of the DeVries Colony at Swaanendael, Lewes, Delaware 1631" by Stanley M. Arthurs.

on this pole they had posted a picture, painted on a piece of tin, of the Coat of Arms of Holland. A native, not realizing how highly the colonists regarded the painting but sensing a new use for the tin, stole the painting and fashioned some tobacco pipes from the metal.

This outraged the Dutchmen, and the leaders of the colony protested the theft and debasement of their symbol to the Indian leaders. The Dutch appeared to be so angry that the Indians, who wanted to mollify their new neighbors, killed the Indian who had taken the tin. In turn, this displeased the Dutch, who explained somewhat tardily that an admonishment would have sufficed. They also chastised the Indians for executing the man, who had otherwise been friendly to the Europeans. This rebuke angered the relatives and friends of the dead Indian, and they decided to punish the whites.

One day after that, most of the colonists were at work in the fields when three Indians, each carrying a sizable bundle of beaver furs, arrived at the log fort, ostensibly to trade. The resident representative of the West India Company welcomed them and invited them into the post storeroom for a bartering session. The Indians entered. Inside, on the floor, a sick colonist lay on a pallet, and a large dog was chained to a wall. The agent followed the Indians inside then went upstairs to a loft where special trade goods were kept. He was coming down the steps, his arms holding several bolts of brightly colored cloth, when an Indian grabbed an ax and struck him in the head. Dying, the trader tumbled down the steps and fell on the floor. A second Indian killed the sick man, and then the Indians assaulted the dog, a ferocious animal that they feared. They shot some twenty-five arrows into it before killing it.

Outside the fort, the other Dutchmen continued their farm chores, unaware of the murders. They were separated over a large area, and most were working out of the sight of their fellow colonists. The Indians searched them out, one by one, and attacked them, either by feigning friendship and getting close enough to strike or by ambushing them. By nightfall all thirty-two colonists and all of their animals were dead. The killing completed, the Indians looted the fort of its weapons, trade goods, and peltry, then torched it.

The Dutchmen who came to Swannendael after the massacre were led by David deVries, an adventurer. He made no effort to punish the Indians. Instead, he quickly reestablished friendly contact with them, and reestablished the colony, this time principally as a whale fishery, and he sent his men into Delaware Bay in small boats in search of whales.

David deVries

It had been easy enough for deVries to make peace with the Cape Henlopen natives. He wrote that he simply bribed them. The Indians had been understandably wary when his ships had first sailed to the cape, but deVries eventually managed to lure one aboard by offering him "a cloth dress, and told him we desired peace. Then immediately, more came running aboard, expecting to obtain a dress, too." But instead, deVries gave them "some toys." The Dutch never attempted to punish the Indians for killing the colonists "because we saw no chance of revenging it," he reported.

There were no additional Indian troubles at Swannendael, and "we began to make preparations to send out sloops to sea (to hunt whales), and to set up a kettle for whale oil and to erect a lodging hut of boards," he wrote.

DeVries had high hopes for his whaling venture. There were excellent reasons why the Cape Henlopen whale fishery should have prospered. Whales were regular inhabitants of Delaware Bay, and they often swam up into the river. To reduce them to oil, the Dutchmen sailed after them in small boats, harpooned them, and then hauled their carcasses ashore where other colonists boiled the blubber into oil. After cruising the bay in December 1632, deVries was so optimistic that he wrote the enterprise would "be royal work, the whales so numerous."

But by April 1633, deVries's ships departed Delaware Bay, leaving Swannendael permanently. The colony had proved less than lucrative. His whalers had struck seventeen whales, but had caught and killed only seven of these. "We could have done more if we had had good harpooners," he wrote. Moreover, the seven whales they had killed had produced too low a yield of oil for deVries's satisfaction. The quantity of oil was so small "that the whale fishery is very expensive," he said. "Having put our oil in the ship, taken down our kettle and hauled in wood and water, we got ready to sail."

DeVries and his men departed, and the colony of Swannendael was never resettled.

Indians Along Delaware
Fear the Minquas

1633

The Indians who lived in large towns surrounded by palisades fashioned from logs on the lower Susquehanna River were known by various names. French soldiers and interpreters, such as Etienne Brule, knew them as the Andaste. Captain John Smith, the Jamestown colonist who met them while exploring the Chesapeake Bay, referred to them as the Susquehannocks. Dutch, English, and Swedish traders, navigators, and colonists who met them along the Delaware River called them the Minquas.

Europeans who traveled from one colony to another spread stories about the Susquehannocks that depicted them as ferocious warriors. Peter Lindestrom, for example, heard Englishmen from Virginia who visited New Sweden tell lengthy and highly detailed (if somewhat embellished) accounts about them. An impressionable young man, Lindestrom made notes of these stories and later included them in "Geographia Americae," his book about his own experiences in New Sweden. Two navigators—David de Vries of Holland and Thomas Yong of England—encountered Minquas war parties during their respective voyages of 1633 and 1634 and recorded their experiences in their journals. The Minquas emerge from these writings as bold and determined men who consistently terrorized and robbed the Indians who lived along the Delaware. The accounts of these explorers make it clear that the Minquas they encountered had little fear of the Europeans who sailed into the Delaware.

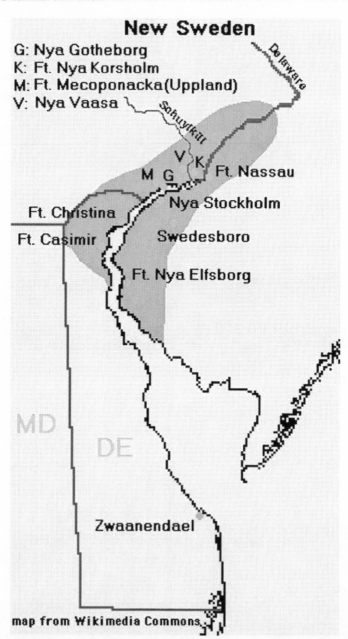

New Sweden

G: Nya Gotheborg
K: Ft. Nya Korsholm
M: Ft. Mecoponacka (Uppland)
V: Nya Vaasa

Delaware

Schuylkill

V K

M G Ft. Nassau

Nya Stockholm

Ft. Christina

Ft. Casimir Swedesboro

Ft. Nya Elfsborg

MD

DE

Zwaanendael

map from Wikimedia Commons

By the time Peter Lindestrom came to New Sweden, merchants there were openly selling ammunition to Indians who had obtained firearms. "Formerly it was indeed forbidden, and agreed, among the Christian nations that no guns, powder or lead should be sold to the savages, but after the English in Virginia had broken the law and first begun to sell guns to the savages ... the Swedes began to sell powder and lead for them."

An Indian could obtain the cheapest gun for 10 beaver skins "and up to 20 beaver (skins) apiece for the dearest," Lindestrom said.

Englishmen that Lindestrom met in New Sweden regaled the journalist with stories of atrocities purportedly committed by the Black Minquas. "It happened," Lindestrom wrote, "that the English of Virginia carried on war against these Minquas." In one instance, a force of several hundred Virginians invaded the enemy territory and camped close to a palisaded Indian town. The English advanced on the town with several field cannon, which they fired at the Minquas stockade. Suddenly, the Virginians realized that the Indians, having surrounded them, were in their rear and drove them into flight," Lindestrom said. The Minquas warriors killed a number of Englishmen and captured fifteen others.

After the fighting had ended, the Indians subjected their European prisoners to an extensive torture that included being forced to walk on fire and having their fingers and tongues chopped off. Finally, Lindestrom wrote, the captors "brought forth 15 bundles of reeds ..., which were saturated in fat. ... They bound a bundle on the back of each prisoner, turned them towards Virginia, set fire to the bundles and told them to run home again." As the Europeans ran down the trail with their flaming burdens, Indian boys chased them and, shouting gleefully, shot them down with their bows and arrows.

If exaggerated, the tale certainly helped demonize the Minquas into an even more ferocious nation of warriors.

In his report for 1654, Gov. Johan Rising discussed the desirability of acquiring additional territory west of New Sweden, including land along the Elk River, from the Minquas. Beyond the reach of Rising's Dutch competitors, such a purchase would encourage increased commerce between the Swedes and the Minquas. "We could ... carry on the best trade with them there," Rising said in a letter written from Fort Christina (present-day Wilmington, Delaware) on July 13, 1654.

The governor saw a great potential for the Indian trade, which could become "the most important thing in the country, if we only had enough cargo to draw the beaver trade ... from the Minquas and (a related tribe called) the Black Minquas." These Indians "buy up both our ordinary cargo and also silk and satin cloths, hats and other things."

The following year Rising reported a major development: "The Minquas ... were recently here and presented me with a very beautiful piece of land beyond the English river." The gift included the region "which we have long desired," the governor said. He remarked that he believed the new territory would be "very suitable for drawing to us the trade with the Minquas."

But this was a future prospect. Writing on June 14, 1655, the governor reported that the trade was suffering from two serious deficiencies.

Firstly, the Dutch settlement at New Amsterdam enjoyed significantly more traffic with Holland than Rising's colony did with Sweden. In consequence, "more ships and more goods arrive there," and the Dutch merchants had more trade goods to offer Indians who came in with furs.

Secondly, though long despised by the Swedes, the Lenape Indians had demonstrated a cleverness at commerce. "If they buy anything here, they wish to get half on credit, and then pay with difficulty," Rising complained. These Indians then carried the Swedish goods to the Susquehanna River to barter with the Susquehannocks. "They run to the Minquas and there they buy beavers and elk skins, etc. for our goods." But there was another indignity: "Then they proceed before our eyes to Manathas (Manhattan), where the traders can pay more for them than we do," the governor said.

The Swedes were afraid of the Lenape. "We must daily buy their friendship with presents, for they are and continue to be hostile, and worse than they have been," Rising wrote.

If the Europeans valued the Minquas as trading partners, they also respected them as warriors.

As he explored the lower Delaware River in February 1633, David de Vries not only found his yacht in danger from huge chunks of ice coming down the river, but also menaced by Indians along the shore. He and his crew had sailed to Fort Nassau, a defense that Dutch traders had erected some years previously in 1626 (near present-day Gloucester, New Jersey.)

On February 3, "it began to freeze again," the navigator wrote, "and we hauled into a kill over against the fort." De Vries was reasonably concerned that a prolonged freeze could trap the yacht. If hostile Indians arrived while the boat couldn't move, his party could protect themselves from inside the fort.

"When we had been in this kill eight days to avoid the ice flow, there came a canoe in which sat an old Indian with a squaw, who brought with them some maize and beans, of which we bought a quantity. ... They hauled the next day out of the kill, and passed between the cakes of ice and the shore, which we could not do with our yacht."

On February 11 de Vries suddenly found himself confronting a potential crisis. The stream was icing up, and the yacht had little free water in which to move.

"Fifty Indians came over the river from the fort upon the ice ... directly to our yacht, into which they could step from the shore, and spoke to us. They were Minquas. ... They came on a warlike expedition ... They are friendly to us, but it would not do to trust them too far, as they would do anything for plunder."

Wary, de Vries decided that as the tide came in, he would take the yacht away from the shore and out into the mouth of the creek. The crew managed to sail a mere twenty-five paces before the yacht became grounded in the shallow water. De Vries had the crew throw ballast overboard.

"When the yacht got afloat, we were driven by the current and with the ice and ebb tide, which was almost spent, a thousand paces below the kill, between two high pieces of ice, which had fallen on the shore. ... We were lying between two pieces of ice with the bowsprit over the shore."

This happened during the night, and when morning came on February 12, the Minquas warriors, who had camped nearby overnight, were surprised to see that the yacht had moved. "They all raised a great shout when they saw that we were driven nearer to the river ... and came running to the yacht," de Vries wrote. "We stood, eight of us, on our arms."

The Indians attempted to board the yacht by climbing aboard the bow, but the Europeans managed to keep them at bay. "At length the water rose so that the yacht and the ice floated, and we were to be driven at God's mercy with the ice, which was our great enemy, while the land was our enemy on account of the Indians." The sailors managed to sail upriver on the incoming tide, evading both ice and Indians. They eventually came to an island that appeared suitable for a haven and tied up along a sandbank on the shore.

"We immediately set about making the mast fast to stout trees on land by means of a rope and to protect ourselves against arrows," the explorer wrote. But these precautions provided unnecessary. The Minquas didn't pursue de Vries, and the next day, which was February 13, some Indians who lived in villages along the Delaware "came before the yacht," de Vries reported. "They told us that they were fugitives—that the Minquas had killed some of their people, and they had escaped. They had been plundered of all of their corn, their houses had been burnt and they had escaped in great want. ... The Minquas had all left and gone ... back to their country."

The weather turned warm on February 14, and de Vries began descending the river and reached his whaling camp at Cape Henlopen on February 20. Although he had explored the Delaware, which the Dutch called the South River, and had survived some colorful adventures, nonetheless "we had failed to obtain corn in the South (Delaware) River in consequence of the war among the Indians," de Vries said. The sailors needed corn for food on their return voyage to Holland, so de Vries struck out for the Jamestown Colony in Virginia on March 6, hoping that the English there would sell an adequate supply of corn and other foods.

The next year, an English explorer, Captain Thomas Yong, sailed up the Delaware River in his quest to discover the Northwest Passage to Cathay. He didn't find it. He did, however, encounter an incredibly bold party of Minquas warriors. In his report for the events of July 28, 1633, Yong said that he had bartered a knife and a hatchet for some eels that an Indian fisherman brought out to his ship in a canoe. The captain had invited the Indian aboard the ship, and suddenly Yong realized that the man was overcome by "a great passion of fear and trembling." Yong asked what was wrong, and the Indian "showed me a canoe a good way off making way towards the ship." The fishermen said the Indians paddling the vessel were Minquas "and that they would kill him if they saw him."

Yong hid the man in a cabin between the decks, got his canoe out of sight, and remained on deck as the other Indians approached. "The Minquas rowed directly to my ship," he said, "and as soon as they got near her, they made signs for a rope, which was cast out to them." The warriors used the rope to secure their canoe, and boarded the ship. Yong's interpreter couldn't translate much of what they said, but told the captain that the Indians said "they were Minquas ... and made signs to us that they were lately come from war with the other Indians, whom they had overcome and slain some of them and cut down their corn."

Captain Yong accepted the green corn that they offered him. "I used them courteously," he said, "and gave them each a hatchet, a pipe, a knife and a pair of scissors."

In turn, the Minquas "desired to see my truck, whereof I showed them samples," he said.

The Indians said they would return to the Delaware River "and bring with them (their) great store of truck of beavers and otters, and therefore they desired to know where we would be" by the time they returned.

The Minquas said that they would come back in about ten weeks, but the Englishmen mistakenly thought the Indians had said ten days. As a result, Indians and Europeans missed their connection.

Treachery Befalls English Nobleman at Sea

1643

Edmond Plowden was an English earl who considered himself sole owner of the lands along the Delaware River, which Plowden had named the Charles River, after the English king, Charles I.

Charles had granted an enormous quantity of land to the earl, who planned to establish the colony of New Albion on it. Sir Edmond had received this charter in 1634 and liked to refer to himself as the Earl Palatine of New Albion.

In Plowden's view, the east and west shores of the Delaware, which he invariably referred to as the "Charles River," were part and parcel of his colony. In his view, the Dutch and Swedes already living there were interlopers and squatters.

In preparation for planting his colony within the realm of the royal land grant, Plowden immigrated to North America. Settling first at Jamestown, Virginia, the earl set about organizing an expedition that would, when the weather turned warm in April or May 1643, travel north along the coast of present-day Virginia, Maryland, and Delaware to his new lands.

When spring arrived, Sir Edmond departed Jamestown on a small ship, sailed down the James River, crossed the mouth of the Chesapeake Bay, and headed for the Atlantic Ocean, intending to swing north for the short voyage to Delaware Bay. The knight was accompanied by sixteen people who would join Plowden in colonizing New Albion. They included the knight's washerwoman and two young pages.

Be that as it may, when the ship sailed into the Delaware and anchored below Fort Nya Elfsborg (near

SIR EDMUND PLOWDEN.

present-day Salem, N.J.) on May 6, Plowden wasn't aboard.

Gov. Johan Printz personally went down to the boat, which was called a bark, and interviewed the passengers and crew. He apparently was familiar with Plowden's grand plan and was surprised to learn that the members of Plowden's expedition didn't have any intention of establishing a new colony. On the contrary, they not only wanted to sell the provisions they had shipped in from Virginia, but they also requested the governor's help in securing transport-ation back to Europe.

70

This behavior—especially when they "asked for ships to Old England"–puzzled Printz and quickly put him on guard. "I asked for their passports and whence they came, and since I immediately observed that they were not right in their designs, I took them with me ... to Christina (present-day Wilmington, Del.) in order to buy flour and other provisions from them," Printz wrote in an official report. "I examined them until a servant maid (who had been employed as a washerwoman by the knight) confessed and betrayed them."

Printz's interrogation of the skipper, crew, and passengers turned up a dramatic account. Captain, crew, and colonists had disliked Plowden intensely and had decided to murder him early in the trip from Jamestown. Descending the James, they came into the Virginia Bay and headed out into the Atlantic. As the boat came "close to an island in the big ocean called Smeed's Island, they counseled together on how they should kill him," Printz said. "They found it advisable not to kill him with their own hands, but to put him on the ... island without clothes and guns."

A quick exploration of the island determined that "there were no people nor any other animals," Printz said.

The renegade colonists calculated that without food or shelter, the marooned knight would only survive a few days. The conspirators put Plowden on the island and began to sail off. Just then, "two young pages ... whom the knight had brought up ... threw themselves out of the bark and into the seas and swam ashore and remained with their master," Printz reported.

Once he determined what had happened to Plowden, Gov. Printz decided to put all the conspirators in jail at Fort Christina, but first, "I caused all the goods they had on hand to be inventoried in their presence."

A few weeks later, an English sloop came into the Delaware from Virginia with news that the earl and his

Model of Fort Cristina, American Swedish Historical Museum, Philadelphia.

pages had been rescued. Indeed, the ship captain even brought Printz a letter from Sir Edmond that told about the mutiny and alerted him to the renegade colonists. "The knight's letter," the governor said, was "written not only to me, but to all the governors and commanders of the whole coast from Florida northwards."

As it happened, the ship that delivered the earl's letter was the same ship that had found and rescued the marooned Plowden, and the captain and crew gave firsthand accounts of the Englishman's misadventure to the Swedish governor. They related that after Plowden's erstwhile colonists had sailed off, the noblemen and the two youngsters had spent three days fruitlessly watching the horizon for white sails. "On the fourth day ... an English ship sailed near by Smeed's Island, so that these young pages could call it," Printz said.

As Printz noted in his official report to Sweden for 1644: "This sloop took the knight, who was half dead and black as earth, on board and brought him to Haakemak (modern Accomac) where he recovered."

Satisfied with this version of events, Printz turned his prisoners, the ship in which they had arrived, and the entire cargo over to the English, so they could take them all back to Plowden in Virginia. "I delivered the people unto him, bark and goods all together, according to the inventory," Printz said, "and he paid me my expenses. ... The principal men among these traitors the knight has caused to be shot."

As Printz penned his report to his superiors in Sweden, the Earl Palatine of New Albion remained in Virginia, where he was still "expecting ships and people out of Ireland and England. He gives free commission to all sloops and barks which come from there to trade here in the river with the savages."

Printz had ordered his soldiers and sailors to stop any and all English ships even if their captains could produce papers signed by Sir Edmond that authorized them to trade for furs in the New Albion Colony. Should any captains be reckless enough to defy Printz's edict, the Swedish soldiers manning the iron and brass cannons mounted on the bastions of Fort Nya Elfsborg had orders to stop them. "I have not allowed anyone to pass by and will not do it until I receive a command from Her Royal Majesty, my Most Gracious Queen," the governor said.

Printz and his Swedish soldiers may have controlled the Delaware by means of the cannons and their forts during the 1640s, but the English stubbornly clung to the notion that the lands along the Delaware belonged to their nation. A decade later, for instance, a Swedish military engineer named Peter Lindestrom and some other Swedes had supper with Edward Lloyd, an English colonist from Maryland then visiting New Sweden. The conversation swung round to the territorial claims of the Earl Palatine of New Albion. As Lindestrom reconstructed the conversation in his journal for June 18, 1654, Lloyd remarked "that the English had pretensions to the New Sweden River, namely, 1. That they had discovered it; 2. That they had it through a donation from King James ..., (and) 3. That Sir (Edmond Plowden) had a special donation of this river from King James."

"We answered him," Lindestrom reported. "If discovery of the country could give it a legal title, then the Spaniards were the nearer to it since they had incidentally been here in New Sweden Bay with ships long before the English." The Swedes made a complex argument, and eventually, Lindestrom said, "this discussion became silent. But then the English commander said that this river ought by rights to come under the protection of England."

The Swedes lost little time in delivering a verbal counterpunch. "It now belongs to Queen Christina of Sweden and it was hoped would so continue," Lindestrom noted.

Swedish rule did indeed continue along the Delaware River, but only for a little more than a year. In September 1655, a Dutch fleet from New Netherlands conquered New Sweden. Nearly nine years later, in August 1664, the English conquered New Netherlands, and the Delaware lands at last fell under English sway. This happened much too late for Sir Edmund, who had died in 1659 without ever managing to establish his colony on the Delaware.

For his part, Lindestrom adds an incongruent postscript to his June 18 journal entry that had absolutely nothing to do with the unfortunate earl or the super with Edward Lloyd, the military commander from Maryland.

"One night on our first arrival at Fort Christina," Lindestrom wrote, "one of our soldiers who had lately arrived at Fort Christina" was assigned to guard duty. Nearly everybody in the garrison had turned in when, well into the watch, the guard suddenly summoned the other soldiers. "Alarm. Alarm. The enemy is about," the man shouted. "Thereupon the drummer beat the alarm," and the entire garrison of sleepy soldiers turned out, Lindestrom recounted. What's wrong, they asked. "The enemy is here close to the fort," he replied. "See how many burning torches there are!"

His comrades laughed, then explained that the flickering lights in the darkness surrounding the fort came from fireflies, not the torches of Indian warriors or Dutch or English soldiers.

Sir Johan Closes River to Control Fur Trade

1643

Sir Johan Printz achieved two distinctions during his eleven years as royal governor of the New Sweden Colony.

The first was significant. Arriving in the colony in February 1643, Printz strengthened the colony's existing defenses along the Delaware River, built several new ones, and then closed the river to ships of merchants from rival colonies. This let Swedish merchants monopolize the fur trade with the Indians, but angered the authorities of other colonies on the Eastern Seaboard.

The second distinction was colorful, but trifling. The governor, who was obese, acquired a derogatory nickname that the Lenni Lenape Indians bestowed on him—"meschatz." The Indian word "meschatz" meant "large belly," according to Peter Lindestrom, a Swedish military engineer who arrived in New Sweden in 1654. "Thus they called him," Lindestrom reported in a book titled *Geographia Americae* that he wrote about the colony. He never met Printz, who had sailed for Europe several months before Lindestrom's arrival in New Sweden.

A decade earlier, David de Vries, a Dutch adventurer, had recorded his impression of Printz after meeting him at Tinnicum Island in the Delaware River in 1643. "He was ...," de Vries said, "a man of large size who weighed over 400 pounds." The Dutchman described the Swedish governor as hospitable. When Printz learned that de Vries had explored and traded on the river years before the Swedes colonized it, he "had a silver mug brought, with which he treated the

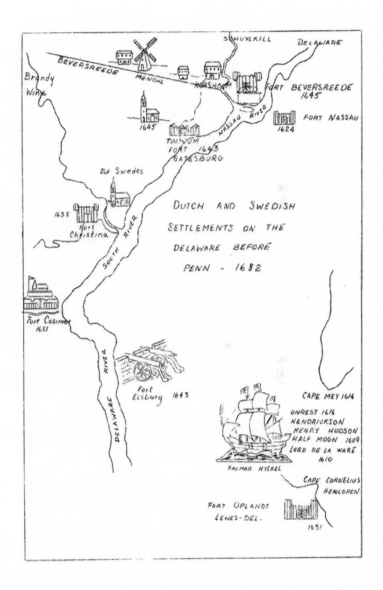

BEVERSREEDE

MENONE

SCHUYLKILL

DELAWARE

Brandy Wine

HORSHAM

FORT BEVERSREEDE 1645

NASSAU RIVER

FORT NASSAU 1624

1645

TINICUM FORT 1643 GATESBURG

Old Swedes

1638

Fort Christina

SOUTH RIVER

DUTCH AND SWEDISH SETTLEMENTS ON THE DELAWARE BEFORE PENN - 1682

Fort Casimir 1651

DELAWARE RIVER

Fort Elsburg 1643

CAPE MEY 1614

UNREST 1616 HENDRICKSON HENRY HUDSON HALF MOON 1609 LORD DE LA WARE 1610

KALMAR NYCKEL

CAPE CORNELIUS HENLOPEN

FORT OPLANDT LEWES-DEL.

1631

skipper with hop beer, and a large glass of Rhenish wine, with which he drank my health."

De Vries, who was fifty years old, had come to New Sweden aboard a ship whose captain knew that the Delaware Bay contained many shoals, but didn't know how to navigate past them in order to sail into the river. De Vries, who had visited these waters previously, knew the way and ably piloted the ship upriver. Sailing along the river's eastern shore, the ship suddenly found itself under the guns of Fort Nya Elfsborg, which Swedish colonists had built near what is now Salem, New Jersey.

"They fired for us to strike our flag," de Vries said in his journal entry for October 13. "The skipper asked me if he should strike it. I answered him, 'You come here by contrary winds and for the purpose of trade, and it is therefore proper that you should strike.'"

So the captain lowered the Dutch ship's flag, which signaled a peaceful intent, and the commander of the Swedish fort sent some soldiers out in a skiff. They asked the captain what cargo the ship carried, "He told them ... Madeira wine," de Vries noted.

The soldiers allowed the ship to proceed upriver, and several hours later it reached Tinicum Island, near present-day Philadelphia. They found Printz in Fort Nya Goteborg, which he had built on the island earlier in the year.

"The governor ... welcomed us," de Vries reported. "He asked the skipper if he had ever been in this river before, who said he had not. How then had he come in when it was so full of shoals? He pointed to me, that I had brought him in. Then the governor's trader, who knew me and had been at Fort Amsterdam, said that I was a patroon of Swannendael (a Dutch fishery) at the entrance of the bay, destroyed by the Indians in the year 1630 when no Swedes were known upon this river."

The governor readily extended his hospitality. "The skipper traded some wines and sweet meats with him for peltries, beaver skins, and stayed here five days from contrary winds," de Vries said.

Born in Sweden in 1592, Johan Printz had studied at five European universities, then served in the Austrian, French, and Swedish armies. Writing in (present-day Wilmington, Delaware) *Narratives of Early Pennsylvania, West New Jersey and Delaware*, Albert Cook Myers reports that by 1638, Printz had attained the rank of lieutenant colonel in the Swedish military. Knighted in 1642, Sir Johan and his family sailed to New Sweden, a colony with land in what is now eastern Pennsylvania, Delaware, and New Jersey in November 1642.

The new Swedish governor arrived at Fort Christina in February 1643. Responsible directly for the government of Sweden rather than the trading company, he brought with him specific instructions to lure the Indian trade away from the Dutch by offering the natives better prices for their pelts. His orders also called for him to gain control of the Delaware River. To do so, Printz swiftly erected new posts: Fort Nya Elfsborg in present-day New Jersey near the confluence of the Delaware and Salem rivers, and Fort Nya Goteborg on Tinicum Island, which is situated close to the Delaware's western shore, a short distance below the confluence of the Delaware and the Schuylkill Rivers.

Erection of Fort Nya Elfsborg began on March 1, and by May 6, the fortification was manned by a garrison of thirteen soldiers and armed with cannons. In late October, when David de Vries and his captain visited this post on their way out of the Delaware, he reported that the fort "was not entirely finished. It was made after the English plan, with three angles close by the river. There were lying there six or eight brass pieces, twelve-pounders."

Soldiers in the garrison were quick to do some trading with the visitors. "The skipper exchanged here some of his wines for beaver-skins," de Vries said.

With the cannons of Nya Elfsborg operational, Printz succeeded in closing the river to ships that he didn't want on the Delaware and won considerable power over the New Haven colony on Salem River. Indeed, by 1644 Printz was describing the Salem River colonists as "our English," and as early as September 1643, some of the leading New Haven traders had permanently left the colony.

Within a matter of months, Printz established the land along the Delaware River as a Swedish colony under the direct control of the Swedish government.

As it turned out, Fort Nya Elfsborg met a dismal end. The Swedish soldiers managed to thwart most efforts of Dutch and English merchant ships to get past it, but were much less successful in dealing with gnats that infested it. According to the Rev. Israel Acrelius's 1759 book, *A History of New Sweden*, gnats —called "myggor" in the Swedish language—bedeviled the garrison. "The fort was afterwards abandoned by the Swedes and destroyed as it was almost impossible to live there on account of the gnats," Acrelius wrote. "It was for some time called Myggenborg."

The nickname appears to have meant "Gnat-burg."

Susquehannocks Use Cannon to Defend Fort

1663

The Jesuit priests of New France traveled far into the interior of present-day Canada, befriended native peoples wherever they could, established missions in or near their villages, and kept detailed accounts of both everyday life and the extraordinary adventures of the Indians.

Over many decades, the French priests compiled thousands of pages with news of events and descriptions of people and places that interested the Jesuit Missionaries of New France. All this information was kept in a careful and continuing chronicle that detailed the fortunes of the Iroquois and other native peoples. It was these priests, for instance, who reported that the Susquehannocks actively interfered when traders among the Seneca Indians, the metaphorical keepers of the Western Door of the Iroquois' symbolic longhouse, attempted to take their furs to the Dutch trading posts along the Delaware and Schuylkill Rivers in present-day Pennsylvania.

Seneca trappers pursued beavers and other fur-bearing animals along the Upper Allegheny and Susquehanna River's West Branch. The Susquehannocks controlled the lower Susquehanna region that Seneca traders had to cross to reach the Dutch outposts. The Susquehannocks, who wanted to monopolize this trade, sought to deny the Senecas access to the Europeans. In 1661 the Iroquois told the Canadian priests that the Senecas, "who carry their beaver skins to the Dutch with great inconvenience and by long and perilous routes," reported that the Susquehannocks were "laying ambuscades for them at every step and forcing them at present to form caravans of six hundred men when they go to do their trading." The Iroquois were eager to begin trading with the French Canadians rather than the Dutch merchants in the New Netherlands, the priests wrote. "They will be delighted to be able to return hence by water, laden with goods for which they are now forced to go a great distance, on foot, to the country of the Dutch," the scribes reported.

These records have come down to us in the form of a large collection of books called *The Jesuit Relations and Allied Documents: Travels and Explorations of the Jesuit Missionaries in New France 1610-1791*. This account of conflict between the Iroquois and Susquehannocks comes chiefly from the priestly records kept for Lower Canada for the years 1662-1664.

In 1663 the Iroquois sent a sizable force into south-central Pennsylvania to destroy the Susquehannocks. They intended to destroy the Susquehannock strongholds along the lower Susquehanna River in the western sections of present-day Lancaster and eastern York Counties. The Iroquois, according to the French priests, raised "an army of eight hundred men" and "embarked on Lake Ontario toward the beginning of last April and directed their course toward the extremity of that beautiful lake to a great river, very much like our St. Lawrence, leading without rapids and without falls to the very gates of the Village of Andastogue. There our warriors arrived after journeying more than a hundred leagues on that beautiful river."

This river undoubtedly was the Susquehanna, and the Susquehannock settlement that the Iroquois warriors found was on the lower river, presumably along the shores of either modern Lancaster or York Counties. The Jesuits reported that the Iroquois found the Susquehannocks living inside a heavily fortified town. Nonetheless, they selected "the most advantageous positions" for their camps and set about working up a plan of attack. As they told the Jesuit missionaries afterwards, "they prepared to make a general assault, planning, as is their wont, to sack the whole village and to return home at the earliest moment, loaded with glory and with captives."

But nothing of the sort ever happened. As they scouted the location more closely, the Iroquois strategists realized that the Andastogue, or Susquehannock, village had been built high up on the bank of a stream, and that this provided a natural defense for the Indians living within the circular palisade. The other side of the town "was defended ... by a double curtain of large trees, flanked by two bastions erected in the European manner, and even supplied with some pieces of artillery."

Inside the wall were elevated platforms that allowed Susquehannock warriors to climb above the village and shoot their arrows over the top of the wall. "Surprised at finding defenses so well planned, the Iroquois abandoned their projected assault, and, after some light skirmishes, resorted to their customary subtlety in order to gain by trickery what they could not accomplish by force."

The Iroquois leaders signaled that they had decided to talk rather than fight with the Susquehannocks. They had decided, they said, that the stockade was too strong to attack and that they intended to go home. In turn, the Susquehannocks said they would permit a delegation of twenty-five of the northern Indians to enter their town, "partly to treat for peace, as they declared, and partly to buy provisions for their return trip. The gates were opened to them, and they went in." But hardly had the gates been closed when the Susquehannocks seized the Iroquois, who were "without further delay made to mount on scaffolds (along the wall) where in sight of their own army, they were burned alive."

This sudden turn of events caught the invaders off guard. To be sure, the Andastogue Indians remained inside the safety of their stockade, but their speakers communicated to the Iroquois warriors outside the gates that the Susquehannock Nation intended to carry the war northward to the Iroquois homelands. "This," they said, "was merely the prelude to what they were going to do. ... The Iroquois had only to go back home as speedily as possible and prepare for a siege, or at least make ready to see their fields laid waste. The Iroquois, more humiliated by this insult than can be imagined, disbanded and prepared to adopt the defensive."

The forlorn and dispirited warriors ascended the Susquehanna and slowly made their way back to their own country. They returned home in late spring to find an outbreak of smallpox that had "wrought sad havoc in their villages, and has carried off many men, besides great numbers of women and children, and, as a result, their villages are nearly deserted and their fields only half tilled." The disease was so devastating that French priests living among the Iroquois as captives reported later that they had baptized more than three hundred dying children as well as an unspecified number of adult Indians.

The smallpox epidemic was the third hard blow that the Iroquois Confederacy had suffered in a year. The previous year, the Senecas and a related tribe, the Agnieronnons, had sent a force of about one hundred warriors to Lake Huron. The expedition had intended to ambush parties of Ottaway Indians traveling along remote rivers, but one morning they found themselves the target of a surprise attack. "Savages living near ... Lake Superior ... made their approach with such boldness that, after discharging some muskets and then shooting their arrows, they leaped, hatchet in hand, upon those whom their fire and missiles had spared." They killed or captured most of the Iroquois. "Only a very few escaped," the French priests wrote. "This shows clearly that these people are not invincible when they are attacked by courage."

Severely weakened by smallpox and fearful of a Susquehannock invasion, the leaders of the Iroquois appealed to their old foes, the French at Quebec and

Montreal "who alone can save them by fortifying their villages and flanking them with bastions in order to defend them against the enemy's army if it should come." To persuade the French governor to agree to this, the Iroquois prepared to send an official embassy to Canada that would "come with beautiful presents and invite us to go again and dwell in their territory," the priests wrote.

French missionaries had long wanted Iroquois children to live with Canadian nuns "to be trained, instructed and prepared for Baptism" in the Roman Catholic Church, and the Iroquois indicated to the priests that they were prepared to send "some of their little girls as hostages," provided that doing so would encourage French colonial officials to send soldiers and European weaponry south to Iroquois country.

Just before the Indian ambassadors set sail for Quebec, an Iroquois arrived with startling news from Canada. He said that he had just escaped from Three Rivers, and the French, aware of the vulnerable state of the Iroquois people, were preparing to wage war against them. Already, thousands of soldiers were arriving from France to take part in a campaign to invade and conquer the Iroquois homelands. French officials had also decided to murder all the Iroquois ambassadors. Any who were spared would be "sent to France to remain in captivity the rest of their days," the Indian said.

None of these statements were true, but the Indian told them in such a credible way that the Iroquois delegation decided to abort the mission, and their canoes never set sail. Instead, the confederacy sent one man to Quebec to determine the truth of the Indian's report. "We received him as a friend, but regarded him as a spy," the priests recorded.

For their part, the French priests who wrote these chronicles showed little sympathy for the Indians of the Five Nations, who, after all, were "menaced ... by three scourges which they have so richly deserved, for the resistance which they have offered to the Faith and the perfidy which they have shown to the Preachers of the Gospel."

The black-robed chroniclers reported that the Catholic missionaries performed many baptisms of Indians who were dying of smallpox victims. This indicated, they said, that God was at work among the Iroquois despite their cruelties to the French clergymen. "Thus the seed cast on the ground bears fruit in its season," the priests wrote, "... and the sweat wherewith we have watered those missions and which we thought was to prove useless is found to have produced an abundant harvest for Eternity."

Fear a Constant in Early Colonies

1671

North America was a dark continent for a long, long time. The early European settlements were little more than toeholds on a vast, unknown and often violent land. Fear was etched so deeply in the minds of the early settlers that their descendants talked about them generations later. Indeed, when journalist Peter Kalm visited the Delaware River settlements in the mid-eighteenth century, second- and third-generation Swedes still recalled, "In the beginning, the danger from the Indians was so great that when the Swedes were plowing, someone had to walk behind the plowman with a gun in his hand to defend him if savages should appear."

The Delaware River colonists repeatedly perceived the Indians as threatening. "All the old Swedes," Kalm wrote, "told me with one voice that in former times the Indians had on several occasions banded together to kill the Swedish colonists, but through God's providence, some old Indian man or woman had always secretly run to the Swedes and warned them about what their fellow Indians had in mind. Sometimes, the Swedes wanted to pay the messengers but they would not accept anything and hastily returned to their own people. The Swedes then collected, and when the natives saw them prepared, they dared not attack."

On occasion, unscrupulous Europeans attempted to manipulate the Lenape into attacking other Europeans. By June 1643, for example, the Swedes had established a colony of 125 people at Fort Christina (present-day Wilmington, Del.), which had achieved dominance on the Delaware River. But an English ship carrying a New England trader named George Lamberton appeared on the river. Lamberton and his company set about buying beaver pelts from the natives. Reports quickly reached the Swedes at Fort Christina that Lamberton was encouraging the Indians to strike at the Swedes. On June 26, as Lamberton traded on the river, Minquas and other Indians grouped before Fort Christina. The Swedes saw that they carried weapons, "which was unusual, and acted in a very unusual way ... as though they wished to scale the wall." Sensing danger, the fort's garrison turned out and "as soon as the people came upon the wall and the constable began to arrange the guns, the savages ran into the woods." Fort Christina's inhabitants had been badly frightened, and Gov. Printz swiftly arrested Lamberton and jailed him for attempting to engineer a massacre.

The official reports Printz sent back to Sweden often painted a dismal picture of the Native Americans with whom the governor dealt. "Our savages," he said, "... become very proud here in the river. I have told them the whole year that we shall receive much people with our ships, but three days after the ship arrived and they observed only one ship and no people, they fell in between Tinnakungh (Tinnicum Island) and Upland and murdered a man and a woman on their bed and they killed a few days later two soldiers and a servant."

Colonists were often reluctant to trust the Indians who lived in the neighborhood, especially in instances in which Europeans encountered misfortune and the situation in some way involved a native. In short, white people were quick to suspect the Indians of treachery.

This was true in 1670 when settlers in Delaware and Maryland learned that Indians living along the Atlantic Ocean had come into possession of beaver pelts and other commodities that had been part of the cargo of the yacht *De Yonge Prins*. Colonists theorized that the boat had become beached by a storm then attacked by Indians who murdered the yacht's stranded crew. The remark of an Indian youth "that the Indians had found a quantity of goods (from the yacht) and had hidden them" reinforced the suspicion.

The authorities dispatched investigators to survey the wreckage and interrogate the Indians. The Indians said that a few days following a summer storm they had gone along the beach to gather oysters when they found "the yacht lying broken on the beach, and the (yacht's) boat in the dunes and a dead body washed up on the beach, of tall stature, brown hair and a very fat belly."

The Indians told the investigators that it wasn't possible to show them the remains of the corpse because a "wolf ate it, and the bones were covered by sand or water." The wreckage of the yacht itself was found strewn along the beach. Under pressure, a few Indians did surrender goods they had taken from the yacht. All in all, the findings of the investigation were so sketchy that it took an official proceeding to decide whether the yacht and its crew had met with foul play or were merely the victims of a stormy sea.

In March 1671 a jury convened at Whorekill in Delaware, reviewed the evidence, and decided that the goods the Indians had retrieved from the yacht and chests that had washed up on the beach had been "wet with salt water." This led to the conclusions that the boat had been lost at sea and that its crew had been "drowned and not murdered."

Fear of an Indian attack precipitated a frenzy in the Pennsylvania colony in July 1686. It was night, and a neighbor boy ran up to Zachariah Whitpaine's house "crying his master and mistress and all the rest in the house were killed, and that the Indians were coming with firebrands to set Zachariah's house on fire," colonist William Markham reported. "Zachariah looked out and ... saw them coming with firebrands. ... He left his house immediately and came to town."

Johan
Printz

1592   1663

The scare proved to be needless. Alarmed, the townspeople waited until the next morning to go out to Whitpaine's homestead. When they arrived in the daylight to inspect the damage the Indians had done, they found that neither Zachariah Whitpaine's dwelling nor that of his neighbor had been molested. What had the boy seen that had prompted both the boy and Whitpaine to run for safety? "I believe they were fireflies," Markham wrote.

Pennsylvania Settler Sold Liquor to Indians Illegally

February 1686

Official records show that a few years before William Penn founded Pennsylvania and Philadelphia, an English emigrant named Gilbert Wheeler was a passenger on the ship *Jacob & Mary*, which sailed into the Delaware River in mid-1679.

The master of the *Jacob & Mary* was Dan Moore, and the old documents report that the vessel "arrived in this river" on the twelfth day of the seventh month, 1679, or July 12, 1679.

Wheeler was identified as a "fruiterer," which was someone who produces fruit. He was accompanied by his wife, Martha; three children, William, Briant, and Martha, as well as by three servants, Charles Thomas, Robert Benson, and Cathrin Knight.

The settlements along the Delaware River at that time were under the jurisdiction of the colonial governor at New York, and Gilbert and Martha Wheeler set up housekeeping on what later became the Pennsylvania side of the river.

Complaints about Wheeler's practice of selling alcoholic beverages to the local Indians commenced within a year. Indeed, a letter dated April 12, 1680, and addressed to "ye worthy Governor of New York," didn't mention any names, but pointedly asked for the authorities to order an end to the selling of liquor beverages to the Lenni Lenape, who had long occupied the land.

William Biles, George Brown, and eight other petitioners bluntly expressed their concerns:

> Whereas, we ye inhabitants of ye new seated town near ye falls of Delaware (called

Crewcorne) finding ourselves aggrieved by ye Indians when drunk informeth that we be and have been in great danger of our lives, of our houses burning, of our goods stealing and of our wives and children afrighting, informeth that we are affeared (afraid) to go about our lawful occasions, lest when we come home, we find them and our concerns damnifyed. These things considered, we do humbly and jointly desire that ye selling brandy and other strong liquors to ye Indians may be wholly suppressed, which, if done, we hope we shall live peaceably.

A subsequent letter from the settlers at Crewcorne, this one dated September 13, 1680, and addressed to "ye worthy Governor of New York," repeated the complaint and added colorful details: "The necessity of our grievances drives us to trouble you once more with a complaint, though unwillingly, against our neighbor, who will not be restrained from selling strong liquors to ye Indians whom he entertains at his house by great numbers and sells it to them by both great and small measures."

Describing themselves as "Your Honor's humble servants and tenants," they reported that the Indians "sometimes ... carry (their spirituous drinks) a little distance from his house and make themselves drunk with it. Then they revel and fight together and then they come furiously and break our fences and steal our corn and break our windows and doors and carry away our goods."

There was a complicating, if incidental factor: Dogs belonging to the Indians also "worried three of our cattle ..."

Should they continue, these drunken episodes might well "force some of us from our plantations, we being very weak at present for resistance. ... Being ignorant of their lingo ..., we cannot appease them when they are mad with drink."

The settlers repeated their April request that "ye selling them strong liquors may be wholly suppressed amongst us by virtue of a warrant from your honor."

The documents don't reveal what action, if any, the governor may have taken. A notation on the September letter discloses that "ye person complained of is Gilbert Wheeler."

Whatever happened at Crewcorne that fall, Wheeler remained on the Delaware. Six months later over in England, King Charles II gave William Penn a charter for an immense amount of land that became the Pennsylvania Colony. The territory included Crewcorne, which appears to be present-day Morrisville.

At some point after this, a young immigrant named John Pidcock arrived on the Delaware, perhaps as an indentured servant of Wheeler's. Although the records don't specifically identify Pidcock as such, the record of a June 1686 assault case—Pidcock was convicted in a Bucks County court of assaulting Wheeler—clearly identifies Wheeler as Pidcock's master.

Pidcock by this time had settled on land along the creek that bears his name at the foot of Bowman's Hill in Bucks County's Solebury Township. He appears to have operated a trading post at or quite close to the Lenape village of Win-na-haw-caw-chunk, located where Pidcock Creek flows into the Delaware. Pidcock squatted on this land and improved it. Documents detailing old land transactions show that this tract was in the vicinity of "the Falls of Delaware."

By now, Pennsylvania had outlawed the sale of liquor to the natives. Shortly after the assault case, Pidcock was back in court, this time testifying for the prosecution that Gilbert Wheeler had violated the colony's law by selling alcoholic beverages to the Indians. Wheeler was indicted, denied the charge, and defended himself against it when the case came to trial. The records indicate that Wheeler was charged with two offenses that had allegedly occurred on the second and eleventh of February.

William Penn outlawed the sale of liquor to the Indians.

A jury of twelve men found Wheeler guilty of selling rum to the Indians on February 11, but the same twelve acquitted him of the charge of selling strong liquors to them on February 2. He was fined five pounds for the February 11 offense.

Court records contain the names of all twelve jurors. None of them were among the signatures on the letters that the Crewcorne settlers had fired off to the governor of New York six years earlier.

Selected Bibliography

Acrelius, Israel. *The History of New Sweden.* Philadelphia: Publication Fund of the Historical Society of Pennsylvania, 1874.

Champlain, Samuel de. *The Voyages and Explorations of Samuel de Champlain 1604-1616 Narrated by Himself.* New York: Allerton Book Company, 1922.

Danckaerts, Jasper. *Journal of Jasper Danckaerts.* New York: Charles Scribner's Sons, 1913.

Lindestrom, Peter. *Geographia Americae: With an Account of the Delaware Indians: Based on Surveys and Notes Made in 1654-1656.* New York: Arno Press, 1979.

Myers, Albert Cook, editor. *Narratives of Early Pennsylvania, West New Jersey and Delaware 1630-1707.* New York: Charles Scribner's Sons, 1912.

Heckewelder, John Gottlieb Ernestus. *An Account of the History, Manners, and Customs of the Indian Nations, Who Once Inhabited Pennsylvania and the Neighboring States.* Philadelphia: Publication Fund of the Historical Society of Pennsylvania, 1876.

Wallace, Paul A.W. *Indian Paths of Pennsylvania.* Harrisburg: Pennsylvania Historical and Museum Commission, 1971.

76290128R00061

Made in the USA
Middletown, DE
11 June 2018